Dr Taiwo Ayodele is a Lecturer and Entrepreneur. He is also a teacher of God's word, committed to discipleship and leadership development. He is a well-known conference speaker, and mentor to various businesses and people. His previous books include *Keys to living a fulfilled life: Concise practical guidance to attaining God's very best*.

Dr Taiwo Ayodele

KEYS TO KEEPING ETERNITY IN MIND: THE MOST IMPORTANT DECISION IN LIFE

Make a Choice: Heaven or Hell

AUSTIN MACAULEY PUBLISHERS™

LONDON • CAMBRIDGE • NEW YORK • SHARJAH

A CIP catalogue record for this title is available from the British Library.

ISBN 978-1-78823-491-7 (Paperback)
ISBN 978-1-78823-492-4 (Hardback)
ISBN 978-1-78823-493-1 (E-Book)
www.austinmacauley.com

First Published (2017)
Austin Macauley Publishers™ Ltd.
25 Canada Square
Canary Wharf
London
E14 5LQ

Acknowledgments

All gratitude to God for His mercies, faithfulness and loving-kindness and for His continuous divine guidance.

Thanks to those that have always believed in what God is doing through me, for their prayers and for their persistent support all the way. I am grateful.

Heartfelt thanks to my parents and siblings for their never-failing prayers, for their care and love.

Table of Contents

Chapter 1
Understanding Eternity

For God so loved the world that He gave His only begotten Son, that whoever believes in Him should not perish but have everlasting life. (John 3:16 NKJV)

If human beings are created for eternal life, nothing could be more beautiful and also more imperative than to discover what it is all about, making sure you can secure your place in eternity by living a life that pleases God.

The concept of eternity seems to be misunderstood by many today, while some are asking, "Where will I be after leaving this earth? What happens when I leave this planet and is there any life after death?" These and many more are questions that run through people's minds today. Someone once asked me recently, "When or How will I know if I will go to Heaven or Hell?" This individual wanted to know if decisions about going to Heaven or Hell will be determined here on earth while still living or after death.

And likewise, many are concerned with the uncertainty of life after death. Hence, this book is timely and crucial for all in order to provide clear understanding from Biblical standpoints and also to gain in-depth comprehension of what the Bible says on this subject. This book will expound the sound Biblical view of eternal life, never-ending life for the righteous, for those who accept the Gospel of Jesus Christ, accept Jesus Christ as their personal Lord and Saviour and live a life that pleases, honours and glorifies God. This eternal life continues in Heaven; while, on the other hand, eternal death, never-ending life is for those who reject the Gospel of Jesus Christ, those who do not accept Jesus Christ as Lord and Saviour, who live in sin and disobedience. This eternal death type of life continues in Hell. Where would you like to go? The choice is yours today.

Eternity means infinity or duration of time without beginning or end. The Oxford Dictionary defines eternity as "infinite or unending time, a state to which time has no application, timelessness, endless life after death and a period of time that seems very long". Eternity literally means timelessness or the nonexistence of time. God is not limited by time, although the whole earth which God created is time-bound, but God is not. God lives outside of time.

In the Scripture (John 3:16) the word "eternal" means life that never ends. It is indicative of life after death and that means that after death, life still continues; in eternity there is no death. The Scripture quotation from John above means that the life we are enjoying now is life in Christ that will be continued after death if we receive Him. What an awesome God we serve. He has built in our heart eternity right from beginning:

"He has made everything beautiful in its time. He has also set eternity in the human heart; yet no one can fathom what God has done from beginning to end. I know that there is nothing better for people than to be happy and to do good while they live. That each of them may eat and

drink, and find satisfaction in all their toil—this is the gift of God" (Eccl. 3:11-14 NIV).

Eternity here also means God's love for us and our belief in Him. He desires that we enjoy our life on earth, that we live in happiness in a continuously fulfilled life.

Another important term that should be understood early in this book is Eternal Life or Everlasting Life. In John 17:3 (NLT) we read "*And this is the way to have eternal life – to know you, the only true God, and Jesus Christ, the one you sent to earth*". Here, eternal life means to know God, to receive Christ Jesus fully as our personal Lord and Saviour. It also describes the salvation that God gives us through Jesus Christ for those who receive Him (Eph. 2:8), trust Him, serve Him and live a life that pleases Him. That life, Christ-Life, which is eternal and unending also relates to the quality of life now and in the future after death. Eternal life continues after this planet:

"*I have come that they may have life, and that they may have it more abundantly*", (John 10:10b NKJV) and NLT version, "*My purpose is to give them a rich and satisfying life.* "

This describes God's intentions about the quality of life He has for us now and after and the extent of His love, favour, blessings and gifts that we should enjoy while we serve Him. Eternal life is also God's own life in us and life that continues after death:

"*For God so loved the world that He gave His only begotten Son, that whoever believes in Him should not perish but have everlasting life*" (John 3:16 NKJV).

11

Through His life we can live, move and exist (Acts 17:28) but without His life in us, we cannot. Through His life, we are blessed with – power, riches, wisdom, strength, honour, glory and blessing – seven-fold blessings through the redemption that is in Christ Jesus (Rev. 5:12, Rom. 3:24). Through His life we have been delivered from the power of darkness and our sins are forgiven (Col. 1:13-14). We can enjoy His divine protection (Ps. 91:1-3) and live an abundant life (John. 10:10b): live a sickness-free, depression-free life and live above difficulties, challenges, terror, accidents, enemies, misfortune, tragedies and premature death (Exo. 15:26, Isa. 28:18, Jer. 30:17, Zech. 4:7, Isa. 54:14-17, Ps 35:1-8, Ps. 68:1, Ps. 91:10, 16, Ps. 102:24, Ps. 108:12-13, Gal. 6:17). Eternal life is now the kind of life each and every one of us must have. This is one of the main reasons why Jesus came (John 3:16) to give us God's life free and forever when we accept Him into our lives and open up to Him how much we need His help. He desires that everyone should receive His unending, timeless, infinite life – life now and life that continues even after death. This is the life that comes with peace, strength, love, joy, kindness, faithfulness, goodness, self-control, sanctification, comfort and much more.

There are other ways of understanding eternal life. It could also mean transcending the power of death. On this planet, everything that lives must die and it appears as if death is the end result of every living creature on earth. But we thank God who set a way (Eccl. 3:11) for the righteous believers in Jesus Christ to escape physically and spiritually (1 Thess. 5:9-10). God from the beginning prepared for us a way of escape from death and this is confirmed and authenticated through Jesus Christ's death and resurrection: "*Knowing that Christ, having been raised from dead, dies no more. Death no longer has dominion over Him*" (John 11:25-26, Rom. 6:5, Rom. 6:9,1 Cor. 15:3-5, Heb. 2:14, 1 Peter 1:3-5):

"*He had in His right hand seven stars, out of His mouth went a sharp two-edged sword, and His countenance was like the sun shining in its strength. And when I saw Him, I fell at His feet as dead. But He laid His right hand on me, saying to me, 'Do not be afraid; I am the First and the Last. I am He who lives, and was dead, and behold, I am alive forevermore. Amen. And I have the keys of Hades and of Death. '*" (Rev. 1:16-18 NKJV).

In other words, it is revealed in this Scripture that Jesus has the keys of Hades and death and these keys were what He used to open the graves of the dead saints who came out from their graves and walked on the streets of Jerusalem (Matt. 27:50-53). So, the keys of Hades and of death are no longer with Satan.

Chapters 9, 10 and 12 will give explicit details about our covenant rights, our redemptive right through the name of Jesus Christ, the blood of Jesus Christ and our authentic power over Satan and death.

Now a way has been set for us. (Rom. 6:23). (NKJV):

"*For the wages of sin is death, but the gift of God is eternal life in Christ Jesus our Lord.*"

As you know, death was not the end of the story of Jesus, God resurrected Him and brought Him back to life. So, in the same way when Christians sleep in the Lord, they will also be resurrected; they will be brought to life –

13

eternal life – life after death, never-ending life with the Lord (1 Thess. 4:16-17, Rom. 6:5).

This scripture passage (1 Thess. 4:16-18) makes clear that death does not end it all and is not the end. That Scripture passage is only relevant to the righteous. So, for the righteous dead the body goes to sleep as the spirit along with the soul is lifted from the body to be with the Lord (2 Cor. 5:8). See also figure 1 – 3 and Chapter 7. When Jesus Christ returns, He will bring the souls of the saints with Him, will raise them as heavenly bodies, glorified bodies, and will unite their souls – the individual persons and the glorified bodies together. This is the comfort and the proof that death has no power over the righteous, the redeemed (Rev. 1:18) because Jesus Christ has conquered death. There is no need to fear death or the future. If we look at the revelation that God gave Paul regarding the return of Christ and the resurrection (1 Cor. 15:51-54), it confirmed what Jesus stated regarding eternal life, eternal death, rapture, resurrection and His return (John 5:24-29, John 11:21-27).

Eternal life is the Jesus Christ's life and it is a never-ending life for the righteous, for those who accept fully the Gospel of Jesus Christ and live as He wants us to live (John 3:16, John 14:6, Rom.6:23, 1 Cor. 15:1-4). This life will continue forever in Heaven, while death outside Christ means eternal death. Eternal death is also everlasting, never-ending life for those who reject the Gospel of Jesus Christ, those who reject Him and live in sin and disobedience. This type of life will continue forever in Hell:

"And many of those who sleep in the dust of the earth shall awake, Some to everlasting life, Some to shame and everlasting contempt." (Dan. 12:2 NKJV).

"And they will go away into eternal punishment, but the righteous will go into eternal life."

(Matt. 25:46 NLT).

Just as eternal life – Christ-like life, knowing God by grace through faith in Jesus Christ (Eph. 2:8-9) is everlasting life, eternal death is never-ending and it is for those who reject Jesus Christ as their personal Lord and Saviour and who disobey God's precepts.

How do you receive eternal life?

Jesus' answer to a lawyer makes it very simple and explicit as we read Luke 10:25-37 NKJV).

Jesus asked him what he understood from the law of God regarding how to receive eternal life and he answered Jesus thus:

"You shall love the LORD your God with all your heart, with all your soul, with all your strength, and with all your mind, and your neighbour as yourself" He said to the lawyer, *"You have answered rightly; do this and you will live".*

We, too, should do likewise and always show mercy on others.

Likewise, Jesus said:

"And this is eternal life, that they may know You, the only true God, and Jesus Christ whom You have sent." (John 17:3 NKJV). Knowing God, to accept lovingly Jesus Christ as our personal Lord and Saviour as the only way to

15

come to the Heavenly Father (John 14:6), the only way to receive eternal life and to enter Heaven (John 3:16, John 14:6, Rom. 6:23).

It is high time we made up our minds and is not this an awesome opportunity to accept Jesus Christ into our lives so that we can receive the greatest gift of all times – eternal life, Christ-like life, life that never ends. Let's follow Jesus' instructions and with our obedience to His word and His instructions by our right actions, we receive eternal life in Jesus Christ and an opportunity of living with Him and the Heavenly Father in Heaven.

Chapter 2
Jesus Who Comes from Heaven

Most assuredly, I say to you, we speak what we know and testify what we have seen, and you do not receive our witness. If I have told you earthly things and you do not believe, how will you believe if I tell you heavenly things? No one has ascended to heaven but He who came down from heaven, that is, the Son of Man who is in heaven (John 3:11-13 NKJV)

If we were to think properly about eternity or other related topics, we must think of them in relation to Christ. The only person who laid the foundation of Christianity is Jesus and He is not only the founder but also, He is the foundation Himself: *"For no other foundation can anyone lay than that which is laid, which is Jesus Christ."* (1 Cor. 3:11 NKJV). Christianity means to be Christ-like, to act like Christ, to be people whose lives emulate Him and whose lives are centred on Him (Acts 11:26, Eph. 5:1-2). So, Jesus Christ is the central focus, the only source, the only almighty, the only creator, the only true God, the founder of Christianity.

If we believe in Him and accept Him (John 1:12, Matt. 6:33), we become children of God whose lives must emulate Him (Eph. 5:1-2). He is the only true God, the sovereign King, whose throne has been established in Heaven and His Kingdom rules over all (Ps. 103:19, Mark 1:15, Luke 17:20-21).

In John 3:11-13, we find that Jesus is the only human being who has ever lived in Heaven before coming to live on earth and there is no other human being with such astonishing experience. This is confirmed in John 3:31:

"He who comes from above is above all; he who is of the earth is earthly and speaks of the earth. He who comes from heaven is above all.

"Jesus who came from above is above all and has the right to reveal, enlighten, expound and describe things about Heaven to us. He is the only one who knows and has ultimate knowledge of Heaven (John 14:1-3).

This same Scripture (John 3:31) reveals that Jesus knew the Heavenly Kingdom more than anyone else who has ever lived on earth. Jesus knew all about Heaven because He is from there and He did not need a near-death experience before He could tell us all about Heaven. And in Matt. 10:32-33:

"Therefore, whoever confesses Me before men, him I will also confess before My Father who is in heaven. But whoever denies Me before men, him I will also deny before My Father who is in heaven."

As we read here, Jesus speaks of the Heavenly Father, God as a sovereign and divine person, who is in Heaven. So, Heaven exists and it is real. This suggests to us that Heaven is a spiritual realm, the spiritual Kingdom of God where those who believe in God, righteous believers, shall meet the Heavenly Father (Ps 103:19, Ps 115:15-16, Matt. 6:9, Matt. 26:29, John 14:1-3, Heb. 11:16). Jesus describes the things that are in Heaven: mansions; the Book of Revelations describes other things that we shall find in Heaven – it has gates and they are of pearl and has streets too and the streets are of pure gold like transparent glass (Rev. 21:21). Who does not want to live in a mansion within a city surrounded by gates made with pearls and the transparent streets made of gold? What a beautiful place to live. What a secure place to live with the Heavenly Father. One should not miss this great opportunity. It is unique and completely desirable.

God wants us to live with Him

God loves us and wants us in Heaven forever with Him (John 3:16).

However, sin separates us from God: "*But your iniquities have separated you from your God. And your sins have hidden His face from you, so that He will not hear.*" (Isa. 59:2 NKJV). This is why Jesus was sent from Heaven to earth to die and pay for our sins and this includes everyone: "*for all have sinned and fall short of the glory of God.*" (Rom. 3:23 NKJV).

Furthermore, Jesus was sent from Heaven to earth to fulfil these objectives:

- To save His people from their sins (Matt. 1:21)
- To preach the Gospel, to rescue the weak, to restore, to recover what was lost, to heal, to offer freedom and deliverance from captivity, to heal

19

and restore, to perfect health and well-being (Luke 4:18-19)
- To preach about the Kingdom of God (Luke 4:43)
- To seek and to save those who are lost (Luke 19:10)
- To save us from perishing in Hell (John 3:16) and much, much more.

Read more in appendix A.

Jesus came with messages of comfort, love and assurance that God loves every one of us just the way we are. As long as we repent of our sins, He forgives us and in fact He remembers our sins no more: "*For I will be merciful to their unrighteousness, and their sins and their lawless deeds, I will remember no more.*" (Heb. 8:12 NKJV). God does not talk about our sins nor remember them anymore. It is only human beings who keep records of evil or the evil things done in the past. We still keep discussing them or reminding ourselves of them, so that we remain guilty and are slaves to such control. God does not keep such records. I remember this statement from a Christian author who said, "It is manlike to punish but Godlike to forgive". It is high time we stop any guilt games or negative portraits of our past because that will distract our focus and growth (Isa. 43:18, and Eph. 4:27). Now, let us focus on the new things that God is doing in our lives and take our eyes off the past and look forward to the new openings and new opportunities ahead of us. We must also understand that no one can earn Heaven through charity, good services, through hard work, acts of kindness or through wealth or connections. And this leads to the most surprising part that most people should be concerned about.

Heaven cannot be earned

One can be so engrossed with several activities and services even in the Kingdom of God that the core purpose of salvation and of knowing God is neglected. This is not to down-play the importance of serving God. It is very important that we engage in "workmanship" with God (Eph. 2:10). Read more in Chapter 13.

And we should continue to render our services to God by humbly serving one another and serving Him through our gifts, living by example, engaging in soul-winning, making ourselves available when needed, developing and using spiritual skills by being part of an active group such as a prayer team, Bible Study team, evangelism team, hospitality, praise & worship team, media team and much more (John 12:26, 1 Cor. 15:58, 1 Peter 2:9, Gal. 5:15). No one can gain Heaven, earn a place in Heaven through church attendance or membership, having daily or weekly communion, good deeds (Titus 3:5), nor by baptism by water and confirmation (Eph. 2:8-9), paying tithes or offerings, although all these are good as the word of God in the Bible instructs us because they have their benefits in the Kingdom. But there is one important thing that will earn anyone who is interested in gaining access to Heaven. So, what we could say is that there is no way to earn a place in Heaven for anyone who seeks to rely on their own good deeds, good characters, church attendance, charity works as the means of earning a place in Heaven or as a means of gaining eternal life. The only way that you can receive eternal life or enter Heaven is through the free gift of salvation. It has to be by God's grace through faith and not by your power or earning it (Eph. 2:8-9, Rom 10:9-10, John

3:3,5). Knowing God and growing in God (John 17:3, John 15:1-8); letting God be the first importance at all times in your decisions or choices in every facet of life (Matt. 6:33); doing the will of the Heavenly Father (Matt. 12:50, Rom. 12:1-2, John 8:32, 1 Cor. 6:18-20, Rom. 14:8, 1 Thess. 4:3, 1 Peter 2:15). This will be elaborated in detail next and also in Chapter 14.

The question now is, "Are you sure if you died today, you will go to Heaven?" So, what is your standing with God? What is your eternal position right now, Heaven or Hell? The Bible says, *"For the wages of sin is death, but the gift of God is eternal life in Christ Jesus our Lord."* (Rom. 6:23 NKJV). If the penalty for our sins is death, how can we then pay for that penalty because none of our good deeds, charity works, daily or weekly communion, church membership or attendance and a host of others can pay the debt? The only way to pay for our sin-debt is through the blood of Jesus Christ and with His blood we have redemption, the forgiveness of our sins, according to the riches of His grace (Eph. 1:7-8, Rom. 3:25-26, Rom. 5:8-9). Jesus died for our sins (1 Cor. 15:3) and paid the penalty.

Significances of His Death and Shedding of His Blood

If Jesus Christ did not die and shed His blood for the remission of our sins (Heb. 9:22), we will not have a relationship with God or even a hope of life after death. The blood of Jesus that was shed on the cross is precious and imperative for atonement and a powerful weapon of victory. Here are some of the significances of His Death and His blood:

- Died for our sins (1 Cor. 15:3, 1 Peter 3:18)
- He became sin, died to sin and bore our sins (2 Cor. 15:21, 1 Peter 2:24)
- Cancelled our sins, all the sin-debt (Col. 2:14)
- Laid down His life for us (John 10:11) and demonstrated His love for us (John 15:13)
- Became the mediator of the new covenant (Heb. 9:15-16)
- Reconciles all things (Col. 1:20)
- Reconciles us to God (Romans 5:10)
- Justifies us (Romans 5:18)
- Purifies us (Heb. 9:14, 22, 1 John 1:7)
- Renders the devil powerless (Heb. 2:14)
- Delivers us from the power of darkness and gives us forgiveness of our sins (Col. 1:13-14)
- Redeems us to God (Rev. 5:9)
- Gives us the gift of righteousness (Romans 5:17)
- Heals us, to enjoy long life and fulfil God's will (Isa 53:5,10)
- Redeems us from the curse of the law (Gal. 3:13) and much, much more.

And through Jesus and by His blood we receive eternal life (John 6:53-56, 1 John 5:6-8,11); it gives us confidence and assurance (Heb. 10:19, Heb. 12:24). Since Jesus Christ's death, His blood and resurrection are vital in gaining eternal life. So, is it not wise to make changes in our lives today? It is not too late to change direction and repent of our sins:

"The Lord is not slack concerning His promise, as some count slackness, but is long-suffering toward us, not willing that any should perish but that all should come to repentance." (2 Peter 3:9 NKJV).

To repent means to ask for forgiveness, to be remorseful about things that we might have done wrong and to determine or make up our minds not to engage in any sinful acts again. Follow David's example when he genuinely repented:

"Create in me a clean heart, O God, And renew a steadfast spirit within me. Do not cast me away from Your presence, And do not take Your Holy Spirit from me. Restore to me the joy of Your salvation, And uphold me by our generous Spirit." (Ps. 51:10-12).

Now, for us to gain access to Heaven and to secure our place there, we need to accept Jesus Christ through faith as Lord and Saviour (Eph. 2:8, Romans 5:1-2) and begin to live a life that is pleasing to God and glorifies Him (Gal. 5:22-26, Phil. 3:10, Phil 4:8, Eph. 5:1-21, Phi. 2:5-8). Accept this free gift of salvation to enjoy a new life on earth and in Heaven since eternal life was paid for through Jesus

Christ. It is ours free as long as we remain in Christ all through our days on earth and do His will.

So, Jesus came to save us from eternal damnation (John 3:16), to reveal the truth that we need to know about living on earth and also about life after death – ETERNITY, HEAVEN and HELL.

The next two chapters will elaborate on eternity, what it is all about and how important it is right now.

Chapter 3
Nothing in the World is Permanent

Do not love the world or the things in the world. If anyone loves the world, the love of the Father is not in him. For all that is in the world—the lust of the flesh, the lust of the eyes, and the pride of life—is not of the Father but is of the world. And the world is passing away, and the lust of it; but he who does the will of God abides forever (1 John 2:15-17 NKJV)

The Scripture passage shows us that nothing is permanent in this world. If we look at technology trends, it is always changing from big cellular phones to mobile phones and from mobile phones to smart phones: from smart watches, smart glasses and lots more. Maybe in the future there will be need for micro or nano smart phones, solar phones and solar laptops.

What about computer trends? There was at first the big frame computer and as technologies evolved, new desktop computers emerged with CRT monitors that changed to LCD or LED monitors. Laptop generations, too, evolved and now technologies have changed. Some are now using tablets of all types to browse, check mails, communicate and keep in touch with friends, family and colleagues to connect with the world. So, all these devices can now connect everywhere, anytime at our convenience and the changes are not over. More creative and intelligent devices are coming especially with the Internet of Things (IOT), where most things may be connected to the Internet including fridges, cookers, cars, etc. Some of the IOT technologies are in existence right now. For example, smart watches – the watch is connected to the smart phone and through the smart watch you can make calls, receive calls and reply to messages and lots more.

What about governance? The government of our nation will not remain here forever: governments will change, new elections will take place; fashion will change, and things in this world will never be permanent. And that is why the saying is, "There is only one constant in this life and that is CHANGE". Understand that as long as we live in this planet earth, we shall continue to experience change.

Another good example is human growth – it is lifelong process of physical, cognitive, behavioural and emotional growth and change. Changes occur from infancy to childhood, childhood to adolescence, from adolescence to adulthood – such great changes take place throughout our life-time on earth. All through those processes, we develop values and attitudes that guide the relationships or choices that we make. In life, change will always be a constant.

Hence that is why the Scripture says that everything in this world will pass away and this means nothing on earth is permanent. But there is a place where everything is permanent – ETERNITY.

Here is a brief representation of what eternity is all about:

"*If your hand causes you to sin, cut it off. It is better for you to enter into life maimed, rather than having two hands, to go to hell, into the fire that shall never be quenched – where 'Their worm does not die And the fire is not quenched.*

And if your foot causes you to sin, cut it off. It is better for you to enter life lame, rather than having two feet, to be cast into hell, into the fire that shall never be quenched— where 'Their worm does not die, And the fire is not quenched.

And if your eye causes you to sin, pluck it out. It is better for you to enter the kingdom of God with one eye, rather than having two eyes, to be cast into hell fire— where 'Their worm does not die and the fire is not quenched.

"For everyone will be seasoned with fire and every sacrifice will be seasoned with salt. Salt is good, but if the salt loses its flavour, how will you season it? Have salt in yourselves, and have peace with one another." (Mark 9:43-50 NKJV).

In this Scripture, Jesus gives us another good example of what happens in eternity. As we have understood from chapter 2 the only person who is qualified to tell us about eternity is Jesus Christ because He is from Heaven and He is the only human being that ever lived that is from Heaven. He is the Omnipotent, Omniscient and Omnipresent God and He is also the Alpha and Omega of all things. This Scripture as told by Jesus is a warning to us all to avoid anything that could cause us to fall into sin, to avoid situations and places that will cause us to sin. In summary, He wants us to live a life that pleases God, to be at peace with all, to avoid sin at all costs through His grace and with the help of the Holy Spirit. It is better to enter life – the Kingdom of God – Heaven with one hand than to go to Hell with two hands. The illustration given by Jesus confirms that eternity is not just a mere existence but has to do with permanence. In eternity, there is no change of situation or position, no change of heart, no change of choice, no development, no growth, no improvements. In eternity change is not recognised and it could now be said, "In eternity the only constant is God". In eternity, we lose the power of choice; we do not make decisions there because everything is permanent. The only time we can make decisions or make choices is on earth but not in eternity. Choice-making or changes of decisions are alien in eternity; we have the opportunity now on earth to make the right decision as to where we want to spend the rest of our lives after this world.

We should understand clearly what Jesus was trying to explain to us that our present existence on earth is an opportunity to help us prepare for eternity. It is on earth that eternity placement will take place and we have been given the opportunity to make decisions on our eternity location – Heaven or Hell. This is the time that we can make a choice since we still have the opportunity to be alive and if we do not make a choice now, do remember that in eternity we do not have the power of choice anymore; we can no longer make a choice or change our choice. No more change of mind in eternity. No more change of heart. Once we enter eternity, we have entered a reality of no change, no going back. It is a place of permanence where our condition always remains the same.

The years of our existence on earth give a great opportunity for us to prepare for eternity, for us to make informed decisions on our eternity placement. I can remember those days at University where after completing second year there was an opportunity to go for a year placement – to make a choice to either go for one-year work experience in a company in the field of study or stay to complete the course without work placement. At that time, it was a choice that each of us had to make to go on a work placement or not to. The same is applicable to eternity placement. God gives us the opportunity now when we can think, when we can make choices, when we can decide where we would like to be after death – Heaven or Hell. God has made the choice available to us by giving us life and to choose life (Deut. 30:19-20 NKJV).

The moment we enter eternity; we cannot change our minds because there is no need of choice. This is the state of permanence, no more change. This is the state we remain until the trumpet calls (1 Thess. 4:16-17).

The time we have now on earth is for us to decide and to make up our minds where we would like to spend the rest of our lives after our time is up on earth. Will it be Heaven or will it be Hell? Which one would you prefer? The fact is we are already making a decision and a choice of where we are going to spend the rest of our lives by what we are doing now based on our choices and decisions. And if they are right and good choices, it leads to the good side of eternity which leads eventually to Heaven and if the choices and decisions are wrong or bad, then it leads eventually to Hell. The choice is ours to make today.

Jesus Christ's desire is that everyone who believes in Him should make it to Heaven and does not want anyone to be caught by surprise by ending up in that place of regret, in Hell. That is why the insights in this book with the Biblical revelations are timely and very imperative for us to begin to discover, realise and understand why we are on earth and for us to start making right decisions and right choices for us to gain access to Heaven.

Chapter 4
Forever! No End

If your hand causes you to sin, cut it off. It is better for you to enter into life maimed, rather than having two hands, to go to hell, into the fire that shall never be quenched— where

Their worm does not die. And the fire is not quenched (Mark 9:43 NKJV)

In this Scripture passage, Jesus describes Hell as a place where the fire is never quenched and the question is, "Why is the fire not going to be quenched?" The answer is, "It is because it shall never be quenched". As we learnt from several Scripture passages and from chapter 3, everything about eternity is permanent. It is forever; it is everlasting. The fire in eternity is forever and can never be quenched. Another important thing to take note of about eternity is the word "worm" and a worm on earth is one of the easiest things to kill. You do not need any weapon to kill a worm; you can just step on it and the worm is dead. However, Jesus describes the difference when a worm enters eternity as little as it is, it will never die. And what does that mean to us? It means that even in eternity a worm will live on forever. If a worm will live forever, what about the souls of the dead? The same law applies to them: the souls of the dead shall live on forever in one of the eternal locations – Heaven or Hell.

If you picture something being consumed by fire and the fire keeps increasing and that thing is not being burnt up and the fire is not reducing but increases: this is what happens in Hell while things there do not die and the fire does not quench. So, in eternity one enters a place of no return and a state of permanence.

We, also need to understand who we really are and what we are made of before diving deep into this topic of eternity. In Gen. 1:27: *"So God created man in His own image; in the image of God He created him; male and female He created them."* Human beings are different from the rest of all other creation because we are created in the image of God. It is imperative that we must not lose sight of who we really are: we are created in the image of God and He Himself is eternal, immortal and invisible – He is a Spirit (John 4:24), He is immortal (1 Tim. 1:17) and He is Invisible (Col. 1:15). Also, as God is a triune Father, Son and the Holy Spirit (1 John 5:7), so human being is also three in one – made up of: body, soul and spirit (Gen. 2:7 AMP). Since we are created in the image of God (Spirit, Immortal and Invisible), we are in His likeness. This is why we have the Spirit of God in us on earth, living in a shelter – the body where the soul – the personality, the individuality resides. On earth, there are no two people with the same soul. So each individual soul (person) has his or her own body as the Scripture states:

"And the LORD God formed man of the dust of the ground, and breathed into his nostrils the breath of life; and man became a living being." Gen. 2.7 NKJV).

"… *then the* LORD *God formed [that is, created the body of] man from the dust of the ground, and breathed into his nostrils the breath of life; and the man became a living being [an individual complete in body and spirit]* "Gen. 2:7 AMP.

To understand this clearly, when the body dies, the spirit retains the soul (the personality, the individual) and since human beings are the only type of creation that are made in the image of God, this is why the spirit and soul never dies. The Scripture states: "*Now to the King eternal, immortal, invisible, to God who alone is wise, be honour and glory forever and ever. Amen.*" (1 Tim. 1:17 NKJV). Since God is a Spirit, Immortal and Invisible as we are created in His image, we are immortal too and we shall continue to exist even after the body is dead. That is why Jesus Christ gives us a deep insight into what happens immediately after death and life in eternity in Luke 16:19-31. He further expounds in detail about two places prepared for the immortal beings after the body is dead. This is why the two places in eternity, where the souls of the righteous dead and the souls of the unrighteous dead will exist.

The Gospel of Luke provides a good example for us to learn from:

"*There was a certain rich man who was clothed in purple and fine linen and fared sumptuously every day. But there was a certain beggar named Lazarus, full of sores, who was laid at his gate, desiring to be fed with the crumbs which fell from the rich man's table. Moreover the dogs came and licked his sores. So it was that the beggar died, and was carried by the angels to Abraham's bosom. The rich man also died and was buried. And being in torments in Hades, he lifted up his eyes and saw Abraham afar off, and Lazarus in his bosom.*

Then he cried and said, 'Father Abraham, have mercy on me, and send Lazarus that he may dip the tip of his finger in water and cool my tongue; for I am tormented in this flame.' But Abraham said, 'Son, remember that in your lifetime you received your good things, and likewise Lazarus evil things; but now he is comforted and you are tormented. And besides all this, between us and you there is a great gulf fixed, so that those who want to pass from here to you cannot, nor can those from there pass to us.

Then he said, 'I beg you therefore, father, that you would send him to my father's house, for I have five brothers, that he may testify to them, lest they also come to this place of torment.' Abraham said to him, 'They have Moses and the prophets; let them hear them.' And he said, 'No, father Abraham; but if one goes to them from the dead, they will repent.' But he said to him, 'If they do not hear Moses and the prophets, neither will they be persuaded though one rise from the dead." (Luke 16:19-31 NKJV).

And this is just the beginning of life in eternity immediately after death:

"*And as it is appointed for men to die once, but after this the judgment,* "(Heb. 9:27 NKJV).

Immediately, the decision is made as to where the departed spirit of the dead will be residing in eternity. This means that our choices, decisions and our lifestyle, our way of life will determine our eternal placement. Choice in this case represents the decision to accept Jesus Christ as our personal Lord and Saviour and live a Christ-like life or choose not to. But those who make the right choice to accept Jesus Christ and serve Him, and devote themselves to the Christ-like life all through their days on earth and follow His precepts will surely secure their rightful place in eternity – "Abraham's bosom" – Paradise -> Heaven. If the body dies, the spirit with the soul will be present with the Lord in Heaven (2 Cor. 5:8). And if they are alive at the time of the "Rapture", they will secure their place with the Heavenly Father in Heaven as Jesus Christ promised (John 14:1-3, Rev. 21:3-7, 10-27). Read more in Chapter 7.

The two important facts we are aware of from the Bible is that Hades is the temporal location of the souls of the unrighteous dead and is also a place of anguish and torment (Luke 16:23-28). Secondly, Paradise is a place of comfort for the souls of the righteous dead and also a resting place from their labours in joyful satisfaction (Revelation 14:13). Those who die in their sins will be taken immediately to Hades and eventually will be judged according to their works by the things which were written in the books and Death and Hades will be cast into the Lake of Fire – Hell. This is the second death. Also, anyone not found written in the Book of Life will be cast into the Lake of Fire. (Rev. 20:11-15).

In 2 Cor. 5:8 and with the aforementioned Bible passages as stated by Jesus Himself, it is clear where the soul of the souls of the righteous dead will be after their time is up on earth. A thorough study of where the people of God will be after death is further explained by Dr Warren. W Wiersbe with Howard Pittman's revelation of Heaven (in Chapter 7) in line with the word of Jesus Christ and the Scriptures:

"The people of God can be found in one of two places: either in heaven or on earth. None of them is in the grave, in hell or in any intermediate state between earth and heaven. Believers on earth are living 'in these earthly bodies', while believers who have died are 'away from these earthly bodies.' Believers on earth are 'not at home with the Lord,' while believers in heaven are 'at home with the Lord.'" (Dr Warren W. Wiersbe, The Transformation Study Bible, p. 1963).

In addition, Pittman's near-death experience seems to give a deep insight into the Third Heaven as well as what happens after the body is dead and the spirit is freed from the body on earth: This is his experience of Heaven:

"Beyond the second Heaven is the Third Heaven (2 Cor.12:2). The Third Heaven is where God's Throne is located, however, God's presence is everywhere (Omnipresent). The Third Heaven is the place from which all the ministering angels are assigned, and it is the place of abode for all the spirits of the saints who have died on earth. No one can travel from Third Heaven to the Earth without first passing through the second Heaven, Conversely, it is also true that no one can pass from the earth en route (sic) to the Third Heaven without passing through the Second Heaven." – (Howard Pittman, Placebo).

He further describes his experience of the third Heaven's homewards trip of saints as:

"… Walking in this tunnel, or along that roadway, or valley, or whatever, was what appeared to be human beings. I asked my escort (Angel) who they were. He told me, "They are saints going home." These were the departed spirits of Christians who had died on Earth and they were going home…I was watching as the saints passed through the way that all saints must take to go home. Here it was, the passageway from Earth to the Third Heaven. I found out only "authorized" spirits were allowed in that tunnel…I realize that these saints I was viewing had not yet received their glorified body because that must wait until the first resurrection...As the saints were allowed into Heaven" (Howard Pittman, Placebo).

In summary, when a person dies, the spirit goes immediately, even as Jesus Christ illustrated in Luke 16:19-31, to that eternal location which is prepared for the individual based on the choice the person made on earth. If the individual received Jesus Christ as Lord and Saviour, and does the will of the Heavenly Father (Matt. 7:21) and belongs to God, the individual will go to Heaven to be present with the Lord (Luke 23:43, 2 Cor. 5:8, Phil. 1:23) until God brings the saints back (1 Thess. 4:14). The Bible calls the righteous (Luke 23:47, Acts 10:22, Rom. 5:17, 19, 1 Peter 3:12), believers in Christ "Saints" (Acts 9:32-41, Rom. 8:27, 1 Cor. 6:1-2).

While on the other hand, those who reject or refuse to receive Jesus Christ as Lord and Saviour, do not belong to Him, their spirit will go to Hades immediately when they die (Luke 16:23-25) awaiting the Final Judgement since there is no repentance after death (Rev. 20:11-15).

Where would you like to be placed in eternity? The choice is yours and you have the opportunity now and the ability to make the right choice now that you can, now that you are still alive. You still have the power to make choices because in eternity as we have learnt earlier, the ability to make choices or the ability to change your mind is no longer an option. Once you enter eternity, everything there becomes permanent and is forever. It is only here on earth that we can still make changes, correct our ways, start making right choices, start living right, acting right and honouring God with our lives.

Think about how you live your life, think about the decisions and choices you are making now. Are they in line with the Christ-like life that is expected of you and do you have Him as your personal Lord and Saviour? Our Saviour, Jesus Christ, is one who came to save us all from Hell – eternal damnation (John 3:16-18), from a place of eternal punishments, where the fire never burns out, where weeping and pains last forever and where people live in regret and in anguish forever. Today, it is worth making the informed and right decisions to re-organise your life, re-address mistakes or errors, to return to Jesus Christ who desires to offer you redemption with the benefits of rightful eternal placement – eternal life in Heaven with the Heavenly Father.

Mark 9:43-48 (NKJV) describes in verse 43 and 45 what it means "*to enter into life*" and this implies: to enter into the Kingdom of God. Life here means the kingdom of God which is HEAVEN. And it goes further to elaborate that if your hand or foot or eye causes you to sin, cut it off. This does not mean that you should cut off your hand or foot or eye physically but it means you should avoid anything that could cause you to fall into sin. The opportunity to live on earth is made available to you by God and the number of years you are given is for you to spend it wisely. And whatever you do on earth has eternal consequences while all your choices, actions and lifestyle will either ruin or enhance your position in the eternal placement – Heaven or Hell.

If you want to enhance your right placement in eternity, you have got to start living and making right choices, right decisions, living right and acting right and doing the things that will give glory to God by doing things that have eternal rewards. Just a thought and this may surprise you: whatever things you do here on earth have an eternal effect. Whether your actions are right or wrong, they all have eternal consequences. So, watch your actions.

Chapter 5
Where Decisions Are Made

"There was a certain rich man who was clothed in purple and fine linen and fared sumptuously every day. But there was a certain beggar named Lazarus, full of sores, who was laid at his gate, desiring to be fed with the crumbs which fell from the rich man's table. Moreover, the dogs came and licked his sores. So it was that the beggar died, and was carried by the angels to Abraham's bosom. The rich man also died and was buried. And being in torments in Hades, he lifted up his eyes and saw Abraham afar off, and Lazarus in his bosom..." "(Luke 16: 19-31 NKJV).

The story of the rich man and the poor man is told by Jesus to illustrate what happens after death, to elucidate on our eternal location immediately after death, to remind us that our decisions, choices and lifestyle on earth will determine our eternal placement. It summarises what eternity is all about since He is the only one who is qualified to tell us all about Heaven. Reading through this Scripture above, we are told that the moment the beggar, Lazarus, died, immediately he was carried by the angels into "Abraham's bosom", a comfortable place or comfortable residence. "Immediately" means instantly, straightaway or right away and not two minutes later or ten minutes later. Also, this is why Heb. 9:27 is vital: it gives us a preliminary eternal decision – where the residency of the person will be immediately after death.

When the rich man died, he was taken immediately, straight away, right away, immediately taken to Hades in torment, in an uncomfortable place, an uncomfortable residence in suffering and anguish. This is still a temporal abode of the unrighteous dead awaiting the Final Judgment (See also Rev. 20:11-15). We can infer from the story that the rich man ended up in Hades where there were torments while Lazarus ended up in Paradise in "Abraham's bosom". The rich man was in torment in Hades, in flames with no water ever to cool his tongue. He saw Abraham afar off and Lazarus, the poor man, in Paradise and cried out:

"And being in torments in Hades, he lifted up his eyes and saw Abraham afar off, and Lazarus in his bosom. Then he cried and said, 'Father Abraham, have mercy on me, and send Lazarus that he may dip the tip of his finger in water and cool my tongue; for I am tormented in this flame. But Abraham said, 'Son, remember that in your lifetime you received your good things, and likewise Lazarus evil things; but now he is comforted and you are tormented." (*Luke 16:23-25 NKJV*).

As we have read, the rich man is faced with everlasting years of torment in flames with no water to cool his tongue. When he was alive, he had everything he wanted, was respected by many because he was rich, controlling things and people and all his servants. But this is the reality of eternity. As soon as the body dies, the spirit is freed with the soul and as we have learnt earlier that the human soul belongs to the spirit – meaning: when the body dies, the spirit retains the soul (the individual or the personality). So, the spirit is lifted along with the soul and returns to the appropriate eternity location based on the decisions and choices (to receive Jesus Christ as Lord and Saviour or not to) made.

Hence why the soul of the individual will be taken to either of these eternal locations, eternal residences: Hades – a place of torment, where its fire never runs out or burns out, a place of those who die in their sins awaiting the Final Judgment and eventually be cast into the Lake of Fire – Hell. At a later time (Rev. 20:7-10), Satan will be cast into Hell but not yet in Hell. Or to "Abraham's bosom" – Paradise, a place where those who die in Christ Jesus will rest and find comfort – Heaven (Rev. 14:13).

The poor man, Lazarus, entered into his eternal residence – Paradise not because he was poor but because he made the right choices and lived a Christ-like life. He made the right decisions to honour God at all times and in all situations. He dedicated his life to God. On the other hand, the rich man entered into his eternal residence – Hades because of his wrong choices: did not receive Jesus Christ into his life while on earth, made the wrong decisions. His lifestyle was not pleasing to God; he did not live a Christ-centred life. He had the opportunities but chose to live a worldly lifestyle. Friends, it is evident from the illustration that Jesus Himself reveals to us that it is the decisions and choices that we make here on earth with our choice of lifestyle that determine our eternal location or eternal residence.

This revelation did not end there. The rich man begged Abraham to send Lazarus to preach to his five brothers who were still alive so that they could learn and correct their lifestyle and make the right choices so that they would not end up in an unpleasant location in eternity:

"Then he said, 'I beg you therefore, father, that you would send him to my father's house, for I have five brothers, that he may testify to them, lest they also come to this place of torment.' Abraham said to him, 'They have Moses and the prophets; let them hear them.' And he said, 'No, father Abraham; but if one goes to them from the dead, they will repent.' But he said to him, 'If they do not hear Moses and the prophets, neither will they be persuaded though one rise from the dead.'" (Luke 16:27-31 NKJV).

Friends, the rich man now discovered that on earth while we are still living, we have the opportunity to repent, the opportunity to change our choices, the opportunity to make Christ our Lord and Saviour, the opportunity to pray to God and ask for and receive forgiveness, opportunity to live a sanctified life on a daily basis and the opportunity to make right changes, the opportunity to obey God, live by faith, demonstrate agape love and live by God's principles, the opportunity to do His will. We have the opportunity to make right decisions and right choices; the opportunity to avoid sin and the opportunity to avoid wrongful or evil associations or wrong friendships; the opportunity to break and stop sinful relationships: to stop wrongful acts, to stop alcoholism, to stop terrorising others or murdering; to stop abusing people or falsely accusing people and to stop any form of adultery or fornication. In summary, we have the opportunity to stop living in sin (Gal. 5:19-21).

The rich man discovered this only when it was too late in Hades – a place of eternal torment. The rich man's eternal placement in Hades in torment leads to Hell forever, while for the poor man, Lazarus' eternal placement leads to eternal happiness in Heaven forever.

This proves to us that we cannot change our minds in eternity because in eternity, life is permanent. There is no salvation after death. Praising and worshipping God is of no use in eternity; Bible study is of no use in eternity. There is no prayer meeting there. There is no Sunday school teaching, no singles' and relationships' seminars. There is no leadership training and there is no preaching in eternity. All preaching, teachings, seminars, workshops, deliverance services, intercessory prayers, prayers for leaders and nations, workers' meeting and training will all end on earth because when our time is up on earth, we shall enter the state of reality where we shall all know God and see Him as He is (1 John 3:2-3).

When we see the Lord Himself in His glory and majesty, we do not need anyone or any Bible study to reveal again who He is because we will see Him face to face. So, all forms of evangelism, preaching and services will end here on earth. We have no other choice than to settle in our eternal location to await the reward for what we did on earth at the appropriate time. (2 Cor. 5:10, Rev. 20:12-15).

So, when an individual is freed from physical body by death, the spirit will go immediately to one these two places:

- Paradise – Heaven for the saints (Luke 16:22, Luke 23:43, 2 Cor. 5:2, 8)
- Hades (Luke 16:23) – Temporal abode of the souls of the unrighteous dead awaiting the Final

Judgement and will eventually be cast into the Lake of Fire – Hell (Matt. 25:41, Rev. 20:11-15)

The word "Paradise" seems to be used as synonym for Heaven (Luke 23:43, 2 Cor. 12:3, Rev. 2:7). Read further in Chapter 7.

The Scripture passage in Deut. 30:19 states:

"See, I have set before you today life and good, death and evil, in that I command you today to love the LORD your God, to walk in His ways, and to keep His commandments, His statutes, and His judgments, that you may live and multiply; and the LORD your God will bless you in the land which you go to possess. But if your heart turns away so that you do not hear, and are drawn away, and worship other gods and serve them, I announce to you today that you shall surely perish; you shall not prolong your days in the land which you cross over the Jordan to go in and possess. I call heaven and earth as witnesses today against you, that I have set before you life and death, blessing and cursing; therefore choose life, that both you and your descendants may live; that you may love the LORD your God, that you may obey His voice, and that you may cling to Him, for He is your life and the length of your days; and that you may dwell in the land which the LORD swore to your fathers, to Abraham, Isaac, and Jacob, to give them." (Deut. 30:15-20 NKJV).

It is clear from this passage above that there are only two ways laid out on earth and we must choose one to follow. Both ways have destinations – best destination and worst destination. And one of the ways is orchestrated by God which is life – eternal life through the acceptance of

Jesus Christ as Lord and Saviour, by loving the Lord our God, following His ways, and keeping His Commandments, His Statutes and His Judgements so that we can live – so that we can continue to exist in the right eternal Home – Heaven at the end of our time on earth. In other words, God's way that has been shown to us leads to Heaven.

While on the other hand, God revealed in the Bible to us, the other way as organised by the devil. This is death, eternal death, as arranged by the devil – Satan. And from the Scripture passage above, those who turn away from God, who reject the Gospel of Jesus Christ (Salvation), who worship and serve other gods shall surely perish and end up in Hell.

It is important to note that we have only two choices of eternal placement and it is on earth that we have to choose one out of the two – and not in eternity. But God Himself advises us: "*therefore choose life, that both you and your descendants may live.*" He desires that we choose Heaven which is the best choice anyway, instead of Hell. Read more in Chapter 7, 14, 17 and 18.

The question to you is, "Where would you like to spend eternity – Heaven or Hell? It is high time we examine ourselves and check if there are things that we are doing that may place us on the wrong side of eternity, Hades – the temporal place for the soul of the unrighteous dead which will eventually lead to Hell. This is a permanent place for the unrighteous, where they cannot change their location, where they cannot change their choice and where they have to remain the way they were in torment forever. At the Final Judgement, the dead, great and small, will stand before God and each one will be judged according to their works by the things which are written in the Books.

Anyone not found written in that Book of Life will be cast into the Lake of Fire – Hell (Rev. 20:11-15).

And the overwhelming evidence for each individual will act as justifying evidence why God is right and just in His Judgment.

Chapter 6

Understanding Various Uses of the Words Heaven, Hell, Paradise, Hades, Sheol, Lake of Fire

What is the difference between Sheol, Hades, Hell, the Lake of Fire, Paradise, and "Abraham's bosom"?

Just to clarify the use of some of these words above as so many have taken them at face value: they have various deeper uses in various contexts and could mean several things with respect to the ways or places they are used.

The Greek word "Hades" refers to the realm of the dead, the abode of the souls of the unrighteous dead as they await their final placement at the Final Judgement. In Luke 16:23, Hades seems to represent the realm of the dead awaiting the Final Judgment (Rev. 20:12-15). While in Rev. 1:18, 6:8, 20:13-14 the word "Hades" is always used with the word "Death". In the end, Death is cast, with Hades, into the Lake of Fire (Rev 20:14). This Scripture reference (Rev. 20:14) makes it clear that Hades and Hell are slightly different as both Death and Hades will be cast out into the Lake of Fire – called Hell. (Rev. 20:13-15). So, Hades is not equivalent to Hell.

But of course, Hades and Hell are not places anyone will be looking forward to going to because they are both places of torment with everlasting fire. We have learnt from

Luke 16:19-31 that Hades is the place of the dead who are not in Christ. The description of Hades is explained in the Gospel of Luke:

"So it was that the beggar died, and was carried by the angels to Abraham's bosom. The rich man also died and was buried. And being in torments in Hades, he lifted up his eyes and saw Abraham afar off, and Lazarus in his bosom. Then he cried and said, 'Father Abraham, have mercy on me, and send Lazarus that he may dip the tip of his finger in water and cool my tongue; for I am tormented in this flame.' "(Luke 19:22-24 NKJV).

Hades is that place of torment, a place of agony, a place of un-ending thirst.

In the Old Testament, however, the word used to describe the abode of the dead is "Sheol". The New Testament Greek equivalent to Sheol is Hades, which is also a general reference to the place of the dead, though some references describe Sheol as "grave". In the Old Testament, there is a significant picture of Sheol when Korah, Dathan and Abiram rebelled against Moses (Num. 16:30-33) and also Sheol is sometimes mentioned in parallel with the word "pit" or "grave" (Ps. 30:1-3, Prov. 1:12, Isa. 14:15, Isa. 38:18, Ezek. 31:15-16). All we can infer from the Scriptures is that Sheol is referred to the grave, the pit of the dead while Hades is a temporal location of the unrighteous dead awaiting their final disposition at the Final Judgment.

Likewise, in Luke 19:25-26 (NKJV):

"But Abraham said, 'Son, remember that in your lifetime you received your good things, and likewise

Lazarus evil things; but now he is comforted and you are tormented. And besides all this, between us and you there is a great gulf fixed, so that those who want to pass from here to you cannot, nor can those from there pass to us.' "

"Abraham's bosom" represents Paradise and is a place of comfort where the souls of the righteous dead will go. Chapter 7 gives further details about Paradise as briefly stated by Jesus Christ Himself.

What about the word "Hell"? Regarding Hell and Gehenna, in the Gospel of Matthew we read:

"And do not fear those who kill the body but cannot kill the soul. But rather fear Him who is able to destroy both soul and body in hell." (Matt. 10:28 NKJV) and

"And do not be afraid of those who kill the body but cannot kill the soul; but rather be afraid of Him who can destroy both soul and body in hell (Gehenna)." (Matt. 10:28 AMP).

The Greek word for "Hell" in the King James Version and in other versions amplified (AMP) etc is "Gehenna" as read in Matt. 10:28. In Mark 9:43-49, Hell means Gehenna – a place where its fire can never be put out. Also, in Matt. 10:28 Jesus is talking of the Final Judgement while in Luke 16:19-31, He is talking about what happens immediately after death.

So, Hell or Gehenna is the Lake of Fire described in Revelation 19 and 20. One thousand years later, Satan will be cast into Hell (Revelation 20:10) and those whose names are not found in the Book of Life will be hurled into the Lake of Fire – Hell (Revelation 20:15) forever. Also, Revelation 20 makes it clear that Hades and the Lake of

Fire are not the same place. At the great Judgement Day at the end of the thousand-year kingdom, those in Hades will be removed from Hades, as Revelation 20:12-15(AMP) states:

"I [also] saw the dead, great and small; they stood before the throne, and books were opened. Then another book was opened, which is [the Book] of Life. And the dead were judged (sentenced) by what they had done their whole way of feeling and acting, their aims and endeavours] in accordance with what was recorded in the books.

"And the sea delivered up the dead who were in it, death and Hades (the state of death or disembodied existence) surrendered the dead in them, and all were tried and their cases determined by what they had done [according to their motives, aims, and works].

"Then death and Hades (the state of death or disembodied existence) were thrown into the lake of fire. This is the second death, the lake of fire.

"And if anyone's [name] was not found recorded in the Book of Life, he was hurled into the lake of fire."

And the unrighteous dead, Hades and anyone not found written in the Book of life will be cast into the Lake of Fire (Revelation 20:14-15).

In summary, Hell is the Final Judgement place of those who failed to receive Christ as their personal Lord and Saviour and whose names are not written in the Book of Life. Jesus Christ came to redeem us and to make salvation available to everyone who is willing to receive Him (John 3:3-5 AMP and John 3:16-18 NKJV).

All the Scripture passages give us the prerequisite of what is required in order to enter into the Kingdom of God – Heaven.

Chapter 7
Paradise and Heaven

"And Jesus said to him, 'Assuredly, I say to you, today you will be with Me in Paradise.'" (Luke 23:43 NKJV).

When Jesus was on the cross of Calvary:

"Then one of the criminals who were hanged blasphemed Him, saying, 'If You are the Christ, save Yourself and us.'
But the other, answering, rebuked him, saying, 'Do you not even fear God, seeing you are under the same condemnation? And we indeed justly, for we receive the due reward of our deeds; but this Man has done nothing wrong." Then he said to Jesus, "Lord, remember me when You come into Your kingdom.'
And Jesus said to him, "Assuredly, I say to you, today you will be with Me in Paradise."' "(Luke 23:39-43 NKJV).

Jesus told the thief on the cross, *"Truly I say to you, today you will be with me in Paradise"*. The man on the cross was saved exclusively by grace as it is the gift of God (Eph. 2:8-9). He could not gain it and did not deserve it but his salvation was personal and secure, guaranteed, definite, assured by the word of Jesus Christ. He had hoped for some sort of comfort and help in the future: "*Lord remember me in Paradise*", but Jesus gave him forgiveness that very day. He died to be with Jesus in Paradise that same day. This may have similar meaning to what Apostle Paul said, "to be absent from the body" is to be "present with the Lord" (2 Corinthians 5:8). The following Scripture passages (Luke 23:43, Acts 7:56,59) further shed light on the righteous dead's immediate presence with the Lord.

Also in the New Testament, the word "Paradise" occurs only three times and each time it appears to be synonymous with the word "Heaven".

First, in the Gospel of Luke as stated by Jesus Himself, "*Truly I say to you. today you will be with me in Paradise.*"

Second, Apostle Paul referred to Paradise while explaining the heavenly vision and revelation he had,

"*And I know such a man—whether in the body or out of the body I do not know, God knows—how he was caught up into Paradise and heard inexpressible words, which it is not lawful for a man to utter.*" (2 Cor. 12:3-4 NKJV).

Third, the Paradise of God refers to the place where righteous believers would dwell – Heaven,

"*He who has an ear, let him hear what the Spirit says to the churches. To him who overcomes I will give to eat from the tree of life, which is in the midst of the Paradise of God.*" (Rev. 2:7 NKJV)

Also, our citizenship is in Heaven:

"For our citizenship is in heaven, from which we also eagerly wait for the Saviour, the Lord Jesus Christ, who will transform our lowly body that it may be conformed to His glorious body, according to the working by which He is able even to subdue all things to Himself." (Phil. 3:20 NKJV).

Likewise, Apostle Paul stated that "to be absent from the body" is to be "present with the Lord" (2 Corinthians 5:8). And later, he says that to die is "to depart and be with Christ, which is far better' (Philippians 1:23). Our Lord Jesus Christ says that those who overcome shall *"eat from the tree of life, which is in the midst of the Paradise of God."* (Revelation 2:7).

According to these Scripture passages, it is clear that immediately after death and according to the illustration of Jesus Christ in Luke 16:19-31 the righteous dead will be taken to Paradise until the trumpet call (1 Cor. 15:51-53, 1 Thess. 4:16-17), while the unrighteous dead will be taken to Hades, a temporal holding place of the unrighteous, awaiting final judgment (Rev 20:12-15). But what activities will take place during the time between death and judgment in these abodes are not revealed in the Scriptures. There are many questions about life after death that go beyond our human understanding. But when we meet our Heavenly Father, we shall know all these mysteries and all will be made clear to us.

The two important facts we are aware of from the Bible is that Hades is the temporal location of the souls of the unrighteous dead and is also a place of anguish and torment (Luke 16:23-28). Secondly Paradise is a place of comfort for the souls of the righteous dead and also a resting place from their labours in joyful satisfaction (Revelation 14:13).

Those who die in their sins will be taken immediately to Hades and after the judgment both soul and body will be delivered into the Lake of Fire (Matt. 10:28, Rev. 20:11-15).

In 2 Cor. 5:8 and with the aforementioned Bible passages as stated by Jesus Himself, it is clear where the righteous dead will be after their time is up on earth. A thorough study of where the people of God will be after death is further explained by Dr Warren. W Wiersbe with Howard Pittman's experience of Heaven as a confirmation of the word of Jesus Christ and the Scriptures:

"The people of God can be found in one of two places: either in heaven or on earth. None of them is in the grave, in hell or in any intermediate state between earth and heaven. Believers on earth are living "in these earthly bodies", while believers who have died are "away from these earthly bodies." Believers on earth are "not at home with the Lord", while believers in heaven are "at home with the Lord". (Dr Warren W. Wiersbe, The transformation study Bible, p. 1963).

But for the righteous we have the opportunity to enter into the Paradise of God – HEAVEN – upon receiving new bodies (2 Cor. 5:1-10, 1 Cor. 15:52-54). We shall dwell in HEAVEN where Jesus Christ says He is preparing for the righteous (John 14:1-3).

Despite various other interpretations or speculations about Paradise or Heaven from different scholars, our standpoint is what the Bible states about Paradise and Heaven as aforementioned. Heaven is our final destination, just as Jesus says,

"Let not your heart be troubled; you believe in God, believe also in Me. In My Father's house are many

mansions; if it were not so, I would have told you. I go to prepare a place for you. And if I go and prepare a place for you, I will come again and receive you to Myself; that where I am, there you may be also." (Luke 14:1-3 NKJV).

Jesus Christ's ultimate goal is for us to live where He lives, to be with the Heavenly Father in Heaven. We believe Him and we are confident that we shall be with Jesus Christ in Heaven because we received Him, believed in Him and lived according to His principles and precepts.

The question whether there are people in Heaven or Hell already is something that some people want clarity on. This means that when the time is up on earth, there is a separation of the spirit from the body. The body goes to the grave while the spirit is lifted up accompanied by the soul because the soul of an individual belongs to the spirit. Human beings are made up of body, soul and spirit – See figures 1, 2 and 3.

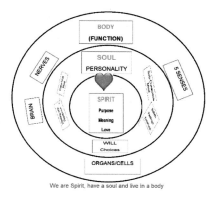

We are Spirit, have a soul and live in a body

Figure 1: Human: Made up of Body, Soul and Spirit

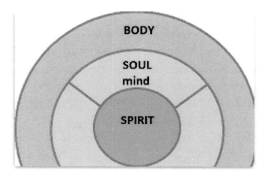

Figure 2: Human Soul belongs to the Spirit

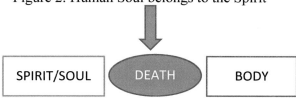

Figure 3: Separation of Body from Spirit (Eccl. 12:7)

And when there is a separation of the spirit from the body, it means that the spirit is lifted along with the soul and the body is separated. It is imperative to note that death does not end it all, but a day of reckoning is coming where we all shall give account of what we have done in the body. There is no repentance or second chance after death. To further understand this separation, Pittman explains it further:

"...we were given a soul to separate us from one another to make us an individual. The animals in this world also have a soul. The only difference between their souls and ours is that our soul belongs to the spirit. Their soul belongs to the body. When their body perishes, their soul perishes with it. When our body perishes, the soul remains with the spirit." (Howard Pittman, Placebo)

As we read from 1 Thess. 4:14-16, those who died in Christ will rise first and those who are alive and remain shall be caught up together with them in the clouds to meet the Lord in the air. Second, the spirit together with the soul of the righteous departs (figure 3) to be with the Lord as explained in these Scripture passages (2 Cor. 5:8, Phil. 1:21-23), while the bodies go to the grave. Pittman provides deep insights into this as he explains what happens when a person dies:

"You must understand the separation of the spirit from the flesh. To know how this works, we must know how we, ourselves, are made. The Bible states that we, as human beings are made in the image of God. To understand this, we must know what God is. God is Spirit; Number two, God is invisible; and Number three, God is immortal. If we are made in His image, then we are spirit, we are invisible, and we are immortal. Therefore, when we look into a mirror we do not see our real selves. We see only the body, or earthen vessel, in which we live. Since we are all made in the image of God, we would all be mirror images of one another without our earthly, physical bodies. Therefore, we were given a soul to separate us from one another to make us an individual.

The animals in this world also have a soul. The only difference between their souls and ours is that our soul belongs to the spirit. Their soul belongs to the body. When their body perishes, their soul perishes with it. When our body perishes, the soul remains with the spirit." (Howard Pittman, Placebo).

This shows that the moment the spirit of an individual is lifted up from the body, then the soul of the individual will come along with the spirit because the soul belongs to the spirit. In other words, the soul is the person's personality – who the person is, the character of the person as an individual. The way to identify the soul after one's spirit is lifted from the flesh according to Pittman's explanation is, "It is one's personality, an individual who retained his or her own personality" (Howard Pittman, Placebo).

Moreover, those who died in Christ now or before the rapture will receive the resurrected body, a transformed body at the time of the trumpet call – when Jesus Christ returns.

All these passages make clear that the soul of the righteous dead will be raised or rather will be raised with transformed bodies and 1 Thess. 4:17 states that,

"We who are alive and remain shall be caught up together with them in the clouds to meet the Lord in the air. And thus we shall always be with the Lord."

The Greek word that has a similar meaning to the words "caught up" is "Rapture" in English, "harpazo" in Greek. In the English dictionary, we read: — "Rapture" means **the Rapture**, Theology. The experience, anticipated by some fundamentalist Christians, of meeting Christ midway in the air upon his return to earth. Meaning to snatch, to seize in relation to removal from one place to another, carried away in spirit. An author states — that the rapture of the church means the carrying away from earth to Heaven.

Likewise, those who die in sin now or before rapture will remain in Hades (Luke 16:23) in torment awaiting Final Judgment (Rev. 20:12-13). So, Hades and all those who died in their sins, anyone not found written in the Book of Life will be cast into the Lake of Fire – Hell (Rev. 20:14-15). This is the Final Judgement. Read more in Appendix C.

Jesus is already in Heaven with the Heavenly Father. Also, Pittman gives a very practical insight based on his personal experience as he further describes his experience of the third Heaven's homewards trip of saints as:

"… When the angels decide (sic) that I had seen enough of the demons at work in this physical world, I was taken back into the Second Heaven just by passing through the dividing dimension wall. Once back inside the Second Heaven, my escort guided me in the direction of the Third Heaven and I was happy at last. After all, this was where I had wanted to go all the time.

Suddenly we came to a most beautiful place. I know that I've already reported how terrible that the Second Heaven was, so you can imagine how surprising it was to find anything beautiful over there. God would not allow me to retain the memory of why this place was so beautiful. I do remember that it was the most beautiful place I'd ever seen. This place looked like a tunnel, a roadway, a valley or some sort of highway... Walking in this tunnel, or along that roadway, or valley, or whatever, was what appeared to be human beings. I asked my escort (Angel) who they were. He told me, "They are saints going home." These were the departed spirits of Christians who had died on Earth and they were going home... I was watching as the saints passed through the way that all saints must take to go home. Here it was, the passageway from Earth to the Third Heaven. I found out only "authorized" spirits were allowed in that tunnel... "I realize that these saints I was viewing had not yet received their glorified body (sic) because that must wait until the first resurrection... As the saints were allowed into Heaven." (Howard Pittman, Placebo).

The Scriptures also provide insights into the Second Coming of Christ when we will be raised with incorruptible bodies, with glorified or heavenly bodies (1 Cor. 15:52-54, Rev. 1:7, 1 Thess. 4:16-18).

Pittman continues his explanation of what he saw in the third Heaven:

"... When the last of the fifty saints had entered into the third Heaven, I started to enter but my escort (the angel of God) stopped me. He told me that if I entered I could not come out and that I would have to stay there until the Father brought me back. The angels told me that all who enter the Third Heaven must remain there until brought back to this physical world by Christ Himself... This fact was testified to by the angels themselves as we stood before the gates of the great Heaven. Dear reader, this should bring great joy to you. There should never be any doubt now. He is coming back..." (Howard Pittman, Placebo).

They chose the right destiny. They made the right choice of their eternal home – Heaven. Why don't you too make this right choice of eternal Home – Heaven today? By living with Heaven in mind and keeping eternity in your heart.

Another crucial part that causes controversy is understanding the timing of the rapture in relation to the tribulation. And that is why one of the most imperative areas in prophecy has to do with understanding the end time, the tribulation and sequence of events as written in the Bible. In the Gospel of Mathew, tribulation and great tribulation are briefly mentioned (Matt. 24:21,29) and the viewpoints pivot around if the righteous (believers or the church) will go through it or will not.

Read through The Life Application New Testament Commentary about "rapture and tribulation" which provides three views:

"This Scripture passage (1 Thess. 4:16-17) provides a clear picture of what is called the "rapture". But Paul does not say exactly when this will happen in relationship to the other great event of the end times: tribulation. So there are three main views regarding the timing of the rapture with respect to the tribulation:

1. Pre-tribulationists point to the period of tribulation (described in Revelation) that occurs before the Second Coming of Christ and believe that the Rapture of the believers will occur before this time of tribulation. They believe, therefore, that believers will be in heaven while the earth goes through a time of great tribulation. This view sees the believers meeting Christ in the clouds, but places his Second Coming as later

2. Mid-tribulationists say that the rapture will occur at the mid-point of the time period of

tribulation. The believers will be on earth for the first half of that time of tribulation but then will be raptured and will escape the last half, which will be a time of intense suffering. This view also sees Christ's Second Coming as a separate and later event

3. Post-tribulationists believe that the believers will remain on the earth during the time of tribulation prior to Christ's Second Coming. Then, when Christ returns in the clouds, believers will be caught up to be with him

While Christians may differ regarding the timing of this rapture, all believe that it will happen and that it will be a joyous reunion of all believers, living and dead. Paul's point was not to give his readers a timeline or a literal description of how all the end-time events would fit together. Instead he wanted to reassure the Thessalonians that their fellow believers who had died would not miss out on Christ's return and eternal Kingdom." (The Life Application New Testament Commentary, p.906).

The question now is, "How is it possible to decide among such varying viewpoints?" Notably this is an important issue as interpretations vary a great deal on this. You can do a self-study on it especially on being "caught up" – Rapture, the sequence of end time events, tribulation and great tribulation. (1 Thess. 4:16-18, Dan. 9:24-27, Matt.24: 21-21, Rev. 13, Rev. 19, Rev. 20). This book did not cover this aspect in great detail.

The Scripture passages, the insightful Biblical revelations, with Pittman's experience give a thoughtful insight into what happens next after our time is up on earth. This book will not go into any form of speculation as it is mainly based on Biblical standpoints and Biblical revelations.

The purpose of this book is to remind you of the urgency of making the right eternal choice right now on earth while you are still alive. After death, there is no coming back to the earth. The urgency of receiving the free gift of Salvation – receiving Jesus Christ as your Lord as saviour (Acts 3:19-21, Rom. 10:9-11). Acts. 4:12 makes it clear that there is no salvation in any other religion and there is no other name under Heaven given among men by which we must be saved. We can be saved only through Jesus Christ and that is the only way to Heaven (John 14:6). Also, this book explicates more on the need to keep eternity in mind as we live our lives on a daily basis, not to forget, nor be distracted of our primary aim of existence – to praise God through our lives, to serve God, to use our talents for God, to please God and let our lives give honour and glory to Him. Also, it reminds us of the importance of knowing God, the need to receive Jesus Christ as our personal Lord and Saviour. And if we have given our lives to Christ before, there is a need to keep growing in God and to live peaceful and holy lives. We have been given only one life and that is the only opportunity to prove that we are capable of using that only life for the glory of God on earth.

The book further reminds us of the need to discover our talents, our purpose in life and the value of services that we are to render to our Heavenly Father while living on earth – the things we are supposed to manage for Him. The questions are, "Are our services such we can be proud of? Are they such that we will be ashamed of when the time to give an account comes? And if we are to give an account of what has been in our care while living on earth including our own lives, will we be satisfied or dissatisfied? Will we be commended or praised as good and faithful servants who will receive eternal life and enter Heaven? Or wicked and untrustworthy servants who will receive eternal death and enter Hell?" This book reminds us of the importance of preparing for our eternal home and using the time that we have left on earth to make the right choices and right decisions and, so, to choose HEAVEN rather than Hell.

This book further focuses on:

- The purpose of our existence: the years of our existence provide the opportunity given to us by our Heavenly Father through Jesus Christ to make a choice on earth about our eternal placement or eternal home at the end of our time on earth
- Being aware that decisions, choices and lifestyle on earth have eternal consequences
- Being aware that decisions (to accept Jesus Christ or not), choices (right or wrong) will determine our eternal placement
- The urgency of making right decisions, right choice and living for Christ
- The understanding of the reality of eternity: it is the final state where everything remains permanent, no more change of heart, no makeup programme. It is a state of no return
- Why Jesus reveals what life is like in eternity: Hades and Hell or Paradise and Heaven
- Why we need to begin to make appropriate positive and right changes in our lives so that we will not miss Heaven
- Why we need to take Jesus Christ's words seriously

- What we need and have to do in order to make it to Heaven
- The Heavenly Father and Jesus Christ desire that we finish our journey on earth successfully and make it home, Heaven, where Jesus is preparing for us (John 14:1-3)

Where would you like to be after your time is up on earth? Heaven or Hell? The choice is yours based on the choices and decisions you make on earth and based on how you live your life.

The most important thing is not to miss the greatest opportunity of our lives – getting into Heaven. We have only one life, one opportunity and it can never be re-lived or re-allocated if missed:

"And as it is appointed for men to die once, but after this the judgment." (Heb. 9:27 NKJV).

We need to make sure we live a life that pleases, honours and glorifies God daily, keeping our faith in Jesus Christ, living the Christ-like life, living according to the principles of Jesus Christ and holding on to Jesus Christ till the end (Matt. 10:22, 1 Cor.1:8, Rev. 14:12-13, Ps. 119:9-16, Ps. 119:33-36, Ps.119:105-112).

Have you come to terms with your sin? Have you decided to repent and make right changes, right choices and right decisions? You cannot continue to make promises that you do not keep and you cannot continue to play games with God by saying, 'Well from now on I am going to do something about my life or I am going to change or be better'. The only way God will forgive you is by confessing and repenting of your sins, accepting Jesus Christ in your life as your personal Lord and Saviour, affirming that Jesus Christ is the only way to Heaven, He who died and rose again; He shed His blood to pay your sin-debt and so that now you continue to live fully the Christ-like life and to do His will. Then your sins will be forgiven and washed away. Now this is a step towards being enlisted as one of the overcomers if you persevere to the end to enjoy your final eternal placement – HEAVEN:

"*He who has an ear, let him hear what the Spirit says to the churches. To him who overcomes I will give to eat from the tree of life, which is in the midst of the Paradise of God*". (Rev. 2:7 NKJV).

Chapter 8

Will There Be Salvation After Death?
(Hearing the Gospel after death...)

The idea of salvation after death or hearing the Gospel after death is something that needs clarification to avoid confusion. Some have this idea that when they die, they will hear the Gospel and be given the opportunity to repent and believe in Christ Jesus but this idea is far from the truth. This idea is based on two statements from 1 Peter 3:18-20 and 1 Peter 4:3-6. Friends, read through these two Scripture passages carefully with understanding and, if possible, with different translations so that you can understand the explanations of Peter in line with the whole Gospel of Christ by not taking them out of context.

"For Christ also suffered once for sins, the just for the unjust, that He might bring us to God, being put to death in the flesh but made alive by the Spirit, by whom also He went and preached to the spirits in prison, who formerly were disobedient, when once the Divine longsuffering waited in the days of Noah, while the ark was being prepared, in which a few, that is, eight souls, were saved through water. There is also an antitype which now saves us—baptism (not the removal of the filth of the flesh, but the answer of a good conscience toward God), through the resurrection of Jesus

Christ, who has gone into heaven and is at the right hand of God, angels and authorities and powers having been made subject to Him." (1 Peter 3:18-22 NKJV).

"He went and proclaimed God's salvation to earlier generations who ended up in the prison of judgment because they wouldn't listen. You know, even though God waited patiently all the days that Noah built his ship, only a few were saved then, eight to be exact—saved from the water by the water. The waters of baptism do that for you, not by washing away dirt from your skin but by presenting you through Jesus' resurrection before God with a clear conscience. Jesus has the last word on everything and everyone, from angels to armies. He's standing right alongside God, and what he says goes." (1 Peter 3:19-22 MSG).

"Therefore, since Christ suffered for us in the flesh, arm yourselves also with the same mind, for he who has suffered in the flesh has ceased from sin, that he no longer should live the rest of his time in the flesh for the lusts of men, but for the will of God. For we have spent enough of our past lifetime in doing the will of the Gentiles—when we walked in lewdness, lusts, drunkenness, revelries, drinking parties, and abominable idolatries. In regard to these, they think it strange that you do not run with them in the same flood of dissipation, speaking evil of you. They will give an account to Him who is ready to judge the living and the dead. For this reason the gospel was preached also to those who are dead, that they might be judged according to men in the flesh, but live according to God in the spirit." (1 Peter 4:1-6 NKJV).

"Since Jesus went through everything you're going through and more, learn to think like him. Think of your sufferings as a weaning from that old sinful habit of always

expecting to get your own way. Then you'll be able to live out your days free to pursue what God wants instead of being tyrannized by what you want.

You've already put in your time in that God-ignorant way of life, partying night after night, a drunken and profligate life. Now it's time to be done with it for good. Of course, your old friends don't understand why you don't join in with the old gang anymore. But you don't have to give an account to them. They're the ones who will be called on the carpet—and before God himself.

Listen to the Message. It was preached to those believers who are now dead, and yet even though they died (just as all people must), they will still get in on the life that God has given in Jesus." (1 Peter 4:3-6 MSG).

What Peter seems to be saying is that the Gospel was preached to those believers who are now dead. However, the key phrases here are "the Gospel was preached" and "to those believers who are now dead, and yet even though they died (just as all people must)". Peter did not say the Gospel **is** preached but rather "...the Gospel **was** preached to the people when they are still living on earth, but now are dead, even though they died as a result of persecution for Christ's sake. Now they are in the care of God and they will "live according to God in the spirit". Those believers who died knowing Christ are saved and they are in care of God. Further, Peter explains why Christians should not be surprised at suffering for righteousness' sake but rejoice that this is about sharing with Christ's suffering and so give glory to God:

"Beloved, do not think it strange concerning the fiery trial which is to try you, as though some strange thing

70

happened to you; but rejoice to the extent that you partake of Christ's sufferings, that when His glory is revealed, you may also be glad with exceeding joy. If you are reproached for the name of Christ, blessed are you, for the Spirit of glory and of God rests upon you. On their part He is blasphemed, but on your part He is glorified. But let none of you suffer as a murderer, a thief, an evildoer, or as a busybody in other people's matters. Yet if anyone suffers as a Christian, let him not be ashamed, but let him glorify God in this matter." (1 Peter. 4:12-16).

Moreover, by humbling themselves at the present time, Christians can be assured of God's exaltation when the time comes, casting their cares on God, being vigilant and, in the end, there is the greatest reward of all – eternal glory – eternal settlement with God (1 Peter 5:6-10).

It would have been so depressing and frustrating in the context of all the vigorous and resounding teaching about holy living through trials and suffering, about the necessity of perseverance in faith, about the necessity of walking by the Spirit, if Peter were to mean that those who have never heard the gospel will get a chance to be saved after death. The question I would have loved to ask Peter if it were so would have been: "If there is such opportunity, why the stress of holy living, going to church weekly, reading the Bible, praying, fasting, spiritual growth, obedience to people and to God, demonstrating agape love and suffering on earth for Christ sake?" The answer is simply, "No salvation after death". There is no such deal: death is literally a dead end with regard to repentance. After death, there is no repentance. Repentance is an alien in eternity. Choices and decisions do not exist in eternity; human power and control do not exist either.

The second idea that confuses people is this phrase "preached to the spirits in prison":

"For Christ also suffered once for sins, the just for the unjust, that He might bring us to God, being put to death in the flesh but made alive by the Spirit, by whom also He went and preached to the spirits in prison, who formerly were disobedient, when once the Divine longsuffering waited in the days of Noah, while the ark was being prepared, in which a few, that is, eight souls, were saved through water. There is also an antitype which now saves us—baptism (not the removal of the filth of the flesh, but the answer of a good conscience toward God), through the resurrection of Jesus Christ, who has gone into heaven and is at the right hand of God, angels and authorities and powers having been made subject to Him." (1 Peter 3:18-22 NKJV).

"He went and proclaimed God's salvation to earlier generations who ended up in the prison of judgment because they wouldn't listen. You know, even though God waited patiently all the days that Noah built his ship, only a few were saved then, eight to be exact—saved from the water by the water. The waters of baptism do that for you, not by washing away dirt from your skin but by presenting you through Jesus' resurrection before God with a clear conscience. Jesus has the last word on everything and everyone, from angels to armies. He's standing right alongside God, and what he says goes." (1 Peter 3:19-22 MSG).

The word "preached" in 1 Peter 3:19 (*"by whom also He went and preached to the spirits in prison"*) can be translated as "proclaimed" and "proclamation" in the English dictionary means "to make a public and official announcement". Also the word "spirits" – pneumata — can refer to human spirits, angels or demons. What could be understood from this Scripture passage is that in between Christ's death and resurrection (no one knows the exact time except God), He proclaimed the triumph of His resurrection to the "spirits in prison" meaning, as verse 20 makes clear, people who were formerly disobedient and who had died during the days of Noah.

It is also likely that Christ was simply making an official announcement of His finished work on the cross of Calvary – His redemptive work and by so doing, declaring His victory:

There is also an antitype which now saves us—baptism (not the removal of the filth of the flesh, but the answer of a good conscience toward God), through the resurrection of Jesus Christ, who has gone into heaven and is at the right hand of God, angels and authorities and powers having been made subject to Him." (1 Peter 3:21-22 NKJV).

It worth noting that the time of Christ's proclamation is not known for certain – either it was between Christ's death and resurrection or at the time of His ascension, only God knows, and Christ's message proclaims His victory over Hades and Death (Rev. 1:18). He proclaims victory over fallen angels, authorities and powers, disarms principalities and powers and makes a public spectacle of them (Col 2:14-15, 1 Peter. 3:22). Christ's glorious reign is over all the evil authorities, principalities and powers and fallen angels that have wreaked havoc on the earth in Noah's days and are still doing so even today. This part is different from "the Gospel was preached to the dead" – meaning the Gospel **was** preached to the people when they are still living on earth but now are dead, as earlier explained. After death, decisions as to where their eternal placement or eternal residence will be, are made immediately as a result of the individual's decisions and choices made on earth: *"And as it is appointed for men to die once, but after this the judgment,"* (Heb. 9:27 NKJV).

But glory be to God who has given us the same authority and the same powers after His resurrection (Matt. 28:18-20 NKJV) with His victory over Hades and Death (Rev. 1:18).

What can we do with this great and awesome power given to us, the redeemed of the Lord?

- Boldness, courage even to preach the Gospel and win souls for the Kingdom of God
- Enlightening people about the importance of baptism by water and the importance of being baptised with the Spirit of Christ – the Holy Spirit, the Holy Spirit who raised Jesus from Death.
- Educating, coaching, guiding people about the knowledge of God, helping them to know God personally, to be obedient to God's word and at the end to make them disciples of Christ – to be like Christ (Eph. 5:1, James 1:25).

Chapters 9, 10 and 12 provide a detailed explanation of the authority that we possess as the redeemed of God and how we can use it wisely.

Chapter 9
Victory in Jesus' Name

"And I am convinced that nothing can ever separate us from God's love. Neither death nor life, neither angels nor demons, neither our fears for today nor our worries about tomorrow—not even the powers of hell can separate us from God's love. No power in the sky above or in the earth below—indeed, nothing in all creation will ever be able to separate us from the love of God that is revealed in Christ Jesus our Lord." (Rom. 8:37-39 NLT).

"I am He who lives, and was dead, and behold, I am alive forevermore. Amen. And I have the keys of Hades and of Death". (Rev. 1:18 NKJV).

The revelation in Christ Jesus as demonstrated through His death and resurrection gives us the triumphant power over Hades and death. So, death has no legal rights over us anymore. And from today through the revelation that we have received, every stronghold of death in our lives is destroyed and we are free from the devil's oppressions, bondages, curses and spells in Jesus Christ's name. Amen.

This is how Jesus Christ wants us as believers to demonstrate the revealed power and authority that we have in Him.

Arise

The devil threatened Jairus' daughter with death. Then Jesus was called on to help:

"Now when Jesus had crossed over again by boat to the other side, a great multitude gathered to Him; and He was by the sea. And behold, one of the rulers of the synagogue came, Jairus by name. And when he saw Him, he fell at His feet and begged Him earnestly, saying, "My little daughter lies at the point of death. Come and lay Your hands on her, that she may be healed, and she will live." So Jesus went with him, and a great multitude followed Him and thronged Him...

While He was still speaking, some came from the ruler of the synagogue' house who said, 'Your daughter is dead. Why trouble the Teacher any further?'

As soon as Jesus heard the word that was spoken, He said to the ruler of the synagogue, 'Do not be afraid; only believe. And He permitted no one to follow Him except Peter, James, and John the brother of James. Then He came to the house of the ruler of the synagogue, and saw a tumult and those who wept and wailed loudly. When He came in, He said to them, 'Why make this commotion and weep? The child is not dead, but sleeping.'

And they ridiculed Him. But when He had put them all outside, He took the father and the mother of the child, and those who were with Him, and entered where the child was lying. Then He took the child by the hand, and said to her, 'Talitha, cumi,' which is translated, 'Little girl, I say to you, **arise**.*' Immediately the girl arose and walked, for she was twelve years of age. And they were overcome with great amazement. But He commanded them strictly that no* one should know it, and said that something should be given her to eat." (Mark 5:21-24, 35-43 NKJV).

"Arise" is the key that Jesus used to defeat death for Jairus' daughter. Many people think death is the final verdict for human beings, the end of life but Jesus once again demonstrated with this revealed testimony that He has got the answer to what human beings think is finished or ended. "ARISE" meaning – I have got the answer in my hands and I have the final say on everyone's life. What He said to the dead daughter of Jairus is "Arise"- it is not the end of your life.

Likewise in Luke chapter 7, we have a similar story of a young man from the city of Nain:

"Now it happened, the day after that He went into a city called Nain; and many of His disciples went with Him, and a large crowd. And when He came near the gate of the city, behold, a dead man was being carried out, the only son of his mother; and she was a widow. And a large crowd from the city was with her. When the Lord saw her, He had compassion on her and said to her, 'Do not weep." Then He came and touched the open coffin, and those who carried him stood still. And He said, "Young man, I say to you, arise.' So he who was dead sat up and began to speak. And He presented him to his mother." (Luke 7:11- 15 NKJV).

In both of these incidents, Jesus responded with the keys He has that He wants us to use when necessary. My prayer is that our lives will not be cut short in Jesus' name and we shall live to fulfil our days on earth in His name. Amen.

"I said, "O my God, do not take me away in the midst of my days; Your years are throughout all generations." (Ps 102:24 NKJV).

Therefore, stand up and start a new life. Such will be the testimony of many today in Jesus' name. Arise to your new beginnings, to a new relationship in Christ, from strength to strength and from glory to glory.

Also, for someone to "**rise**" it means that that person is lying down, sitting, kneeling or in a position where they cannot help themselves at all. And the one who could help that person must be someone who is standing or already has all it takes to help the person in terms of stamina, strength or spiritual power.

If you look around, we can see that many are plagued with death, sickness, disease, joblessness, alcoholism, broken hearts, insecurity, fear, tragedies, misfortune, financial problems, divorce, relationship instability, depression, hurt, pain and lots more. However, Jesus is saying to us today and pronouncing His final verdict on our lives and situations: He says ARISE from all the things that keep us from living a Christ-like life by protecting us from all the assaults of Satan (Rev. 5:1-5). Jesus is the Lion of the Tribe of Judah and He has prevailed by dying and making atonement for our sins. He destroyed death; hence that is why He obtained the keys of Hades and of death.

So, do not allow any form of fear in your life because it is Jesus who now has the final say regarding how long we live on earth. Take the bold step of faith and rebuke the fear of death.

"I shall not die, but live, and declare the works of the Lord." (Ps118:17 NKJV) and also

"...*Because I live, you also will live*" (John 14:19 NKJV), because Jesus lives, I (your name) will live also in Jesus Christ's name. Amen.

Death will no longer have any hold in our lives again in Jesus' name. Amen.

Chapter 10
Keys of Hades and Death: With Jesus Christ

I am He who lives, and was dead, and behold, I am alive forevermore. Amen. And I have the keys of Hades and of Death. (Rev. 1:18 NKJV)

This Scripture verse explicitly confirms to us that indeed Jesus Christ died but rose again and He now lives forever. Now, He has the keys of Hades and death, so death has no power over us anymore because Jesus has redeemed us through His blood and now death has no legal right over us. The keys that Jesus had were what He used to open the graves of the dead saints who came out from their graves and walked on the streets of Jerusalem (Matt. 27:50-53).

Likewise, we read in the Gospel of John:

"So when Jesus had received the sour wine, He said, "It is finished!" And bowing His head, He gave up His spirit." (John 19:30 NKJV).

When Jesus gave up His Spirit, He said, "It is finished". He meant He has finished the work of redemption, He has defeated the devil. He has legally got the keys of Hades and death through His blood that was shed on the cross of

Calvary. He has paid all our debts and now we live a redeemed life, a new, glorious life. This Christ-like life is exempt from eternal death and Hell through our willingness to repent of our sins and sinful ways. And then there is our decision to accept Jesus Christ as our personal Lord and Saviour and that gives us the ability to live a life that honours and pleases God always. We realise that the reason for the action of Jesus above is made clear here. The Epistle to the Hebrews makes it clear as well:

"Inasmuch then as the children have partaken of flesh and blood, He Himself likewise shared in the same, that through death He might destroy him who had the power of death, that is, the devil." (Heb. 2:14 NKJV).

Hence, when Jesus gave up His Spirit, the devil gave up the keys of Hades and death. Now, the keys are no longer with the devil. We see now why the devil has no legal rights in determining the number of our days in this earth because he is no longer in charge; he lost the power over us over two thousand years ago. This is demonstrated clearly in Col. 2:15 and also in Matt. 27:50-53:

"Having disarmed principalities and powers, He made a public spectacle of them, triumphing over them in it." (Col. 2:15 NKJV).

Jesus defeated Satan publicly as through His Death the grave doors were opened and the saints who were dead came out and walked on the streets of Jerusalem (Matt. 27:50-53).

This was a great public display that demonstrates the mystery that Jesus overcame the devil and this proved that death had no power over Him and over us. This also shows that Jesus had the keys, as Paul explained in Col. 2:15. This refers to the public shame that the devil suffered when Jesus defeated him and when keys of Hades and death were given to Him. We shall overcome evil oppression, pain, setback, tragedy, sickness or trouble, and anything representing death in our lives from today in Jesus' name. Amen.

Now, Satan no longer has any say with regards to how long we live. The keys are now in the hands of Jesus Christ – Our Saviour. This is why Jesus made this declaration after the resurrection to confirm that He had all powers, all authority that we all need to overcome the evil world and the devil as we read in Matt. 28:18-19.

The keys, powers and all authority are held in our favour and for our use to subdue and overcome the devil and any challenges we may face on earth.

Why not declare today:

"I understand clearly that Jesus has the keys of Hades and of death and all powers and authority, so, Satan, I am a child of God who has received power and authority through Jesus Christ who shed His blood on the cross of Calvary. I declare today, Satan, in the name of Jesus Christ you cannot kill me. You cannot take me in the midst of my days, I cancel and destroy the power of untimely death in Jesus Christ's name. Amen. I also declare with Psalm. 118:17 (NKJV) – '*I shall not die, but live, And declare the works of the LORD.*'

This I believe:

'I said, 'O my God, Do not take me away in the midst of my days; Your years are throughout all generations.' (Ps. 102:24 NKJV).

I will live to a good old age in Jesus Christ's name. Amen."

Chapter 11

Prerequisites and Correct Use of the Authority in Jesus Christ

"... *who being the brightness of His glory and the express image of His person, and upholding all things by the word of His power, when He had by Himself purged our sins, sat down at the right hand of the Majesty on high.*" (Heb. 1:3 NKJV)

There are prerequisites that we believers need to meet in order to be able to use the authority made available in Christ Jesus. In addition, another imperative is how we as believers in Christ should correctly use the authority that Jesus Christ gives us. It must not be abused nor misused as the authority entrusted to us by God through Jesus Christ must be used appropriately with humility, in obedience, in love, in faith, in sanctification and with a clean and pure heart:

These are a few perquisites that are very important, although there are more:

- Be Christ's disciples. (John 3:3,5,7, John 10:25-28)
- Be able to let go of things that can hinder us from following Christ. (1 John 2:15-17)

- Be determined, be willing and available, creating time for Him, ready to take responsibilities for ourselves and not blaming others for our actions or decisions. (Luke 14:25-27)
- Not engage in things that do not glorify God (Ps. 1:1) but embrace the new Christ-like life. (Ps. 1:2-3, 2 Cor. 5:17, Eph. 5:1-2)
- Be obedient to God: by doing what Christ said we should be doing according to His word (Matt. 28:18-20) and living a life that honours and pleases God (1 Sam 15:22, Matt. 17:5, Rom. 8:6-8, Heb. 11:5, Heb. 13:15-16). Not doing our own thing for our own pleasures only. (Joshua 1:8, Deut. 28:1, Phil. 2:1-8)
- Stay in contact with Jesus Christ often, communicate daily & often with our Heavenly Father (John 14:13) engaging in effective and fervent prayer (James 5:16). Daniel prayed three times daily (Dan. 6:10), King David prayed in the morning, noon and at evening (Ps. 55:17). See the prayer life of Jesus Christ as well. (Mark. 1:35, Matt. 6:9-13, 14:23, Luke 6:12)
- Live a life of faith. (Heb. 11:1, 6, 2 Cor. 5:7, 1 John 5:5, 13, Gal. 2:20).
- Be skilful in the use of our weapons. Be aware that we are in a world at war and our weapons that are not "carnal" or not tangible are: the Name of Jesus − (Phil. 2:10-11), the Word of God − Bible (Heb. 4:12, Jer. 23:29), the Blood of Jesus (Rev. 12:11)
- Understand the Word of God − we should have deep knowledge of the Word of God in order to apply it properly. (Hos. 4:6, Ps. 119:105, Ps. 119:130)

- Operate only with the authority of Jesus Christ. We cannot operate on our own strength or with our own authority. That will never work. Always remember whose authority we are operating from…only IN THE NAME OF JESUS CHRIST. (John 15:4-8, Acts 19:11-17)
- Be part of God's assembly, an assembly of other believers. (Heb. 10:25)
- Always show AGAPE LOVE TO ALL. (1 Cor. 13:1-8)
- Be HOLY AND PURE. (Lev. 11:45, Mat. 6:33, Rom. 12:1-2, 1 Cor. 6:15-20, 2 Cor. 6:14-18, Heb. 12:14, 1 Peter 1:15-16)

The appropriate use of Christ's Authority for a Believer

Jesus Christ's authority is entrusted to us by God through Christ **Himself** but it should be used appropriately and correctly. As we have learnt previously how Jesus demonstrated and used His authority on earth, we should follow the same example; He is our role model. The following basic key principles should be our guide in the appropriate use of Christ's authority:

- It should be used for the purpose for which it had been made available to us. It is for God's Kingdom and not for showing-off and not for self-glorification. Jesus Christ warned against this in Luke 10:17-20 and Jesus refused to show-off when asked by the Scribes and Pharisees for a sign (Matt. 12:38-39). So it must be used in humility.
- The authority of Christ given to us believers should not be used outside of God's will and should not

conflict with the word of God. An example is that of the seven sons of Sceva in Acts. 19:13-17. They were overpowered by evil spirits because they had no personal relationship with Jesus Christ and they had not make a clean break with sin. They were practising exorcism and were trying to use the name of Jesus Christ to cast out evil spirits. The brothers did not realise that Paul's power is from God's Holy Spirit, not from incantations or magic formulae. So, the authority and power of Jesus Christ made available to us must not be used outside of God's will and must not conflict with God's word.

- Discernment is imperative in the use of the authority of Christ. (Eph. 5:10, Heb. 4:12, Heb. 5:14). We should know when to use it and when not to.

- Using the authority of Jesus Christ should involve a fasting life (Isa. 58:6-8), a disciplined life and a prayerful and holy life, being hearers and doers of the word of God, rightfully applying the word of God (Dan. 1:8, Mark 1:35, 1 Peter 1:16, James 1:25).

- We should demonstrate agape love and compassion. Jesus showed love and exercised compassion on people. (Matt. 15:32, Matt. 8:3, Luke 7:13, Mark 6:34, Heb. 4:15).

- The authority of Christ flows through His Word, the Word of His Power (Heb. 1:3) and from daily meditation (Joshua 1:8) and also from daily declaration of the word of God (Prov. 18:21, Isa. 54:17, Matt. 4:3-11).

These are just a few ways to appropriate the use of the authority of Jesus Christ, although there are other areas such as: the use of His authority in deliverances, over oppressions, over Satanic attacks and much more. We have learnt how Jesus Christ demonstrated His authority (chapter 9, 10 and 12): that is the same way we believers must exercise our authority over evil, wickedness, pain, sickness, diseases, attacks, setbacks, tragedy, challenges and difficulties, over demons and Satan. We do this using the weapons that are made available to us through Jesus Christ (2 Cor. 10:4-5, Eph. 6:10-18, Gal. 6:17, Rom. 8:37).

And what are these weapons that we need to know how to use in everyday life? They are:

- ✓ the Name of Jesus – (Phil. 2:10-11)
- ✓ the Word of God – (Heb. 4:12, Jer. 23:29) and
- ✓ the Blood of Jesus – (Rev. 12:11)

The devil or Satan has no answers to these weapons. If we use them appropriately when we are faced with any form of danger or difficulties anywhere, we are safe with these weapons as expounded further in the following Scripture passages: Prov. 18:10, Phil. 2:10-11, Heb. 4:12, Jer. 23:29, Heb. 1:3, Rev. 12:11).

Through the authority in Jesus Christ as made available to the believers we are always protected and safe from any situation we face. We need only to be obedient and be strong; we must learn to use our authority through Jesus Christ and whatever we ask for will be made available whenever we use our God-given authority wisely and correctly:

"And I will give you the keys of the kingdom of heaven, and whatever you bind on earth will be bound in heaven, and whatever you loose on earth will be loosed in heaven." (Matt. 16:19 NKJV).

So, whatever we ask God to stop if it is His will, He will stop. Whatever we want God to do if it is His will for us, He will do it. If we want Him to heal, deliver, promote, bless grant us a peaceful and happy relationship, bless our marriage, be successful, God will grant us as long as it is within His perfect will and timing for our lives (John 2:4, Eph. 1:11, Heb. 4:4-5, Ps. 115:3, Prov. 19:21, Prov. 29:11, Eccl. 3:1, Isa. 40:31).

Please understand that God has the final say over our lives and destiny.

Chapter 12
Your Authority in God

"And Jesus came and spoke to them, saying, 'All authority has been given to Me in heaven and on earth.'" (Matt. 28:18 NKJV)

One of the most astounding teachings in the Bible is about the believer's authority in the spiritual realm, which eventually affects what we see in the natural realm on earth. The word "authority" means permission, privilege, power, rule, control and influence. When people claim to have authority that means they have the right, the control and power over something or over people or domain. They have responsibility beyond the norm. They are able to determine things, to decide things, to render judgments, to exert certain rights and privileges. For example, in the government there are authorities; in the schools there are authorities; in business, in our cities or communities, at the airports, workplace; in transport and in any facet of life there are authorities. These are the people who have the privilege, the power, the permission to set the rules, to determine decisions and judgments.

But there is one who has authority that surpasses all other authorities:

"*And Jesus came and spoke to them, saying, 'All authority has been given to Me in heaven and on earth'*" (Matt. 28:18 NKJV).

After the resurrection of Jesus Christ came this proclamation that He has got all the authority both in Heaven and on earth after defeating the devil in public show (Col. 2:14-15). He also has the keys of Hades and death (Heb. 2:14, Rev. 1:18). Jesus has what it takes to reign, to rule, to exert rights, to control, to permit, disapprove, to open doors or close doors, to judge; no one can question His judgement because His authority and powers are unlimited. The good news today is that anyone who believes in God has been given the same authority through the name of Jesus (Phil. 2:10-11).

Jesus has given this authority to us, believers (Luke 9:1-2, Luke 10:19, Mark 16:17-18).

These Scripture passages above clearly affirm Jesus' desire for those who are His disciples, His followers and believers, to have His full authority and powers. But we have to use them wisely and appropriately.

Where did Christ's Authority come from?

Jesus' authority came from the Father as God filled Him with His Spirit (Matt. 3:16-17, John 17:1-2, Phil. 2:8-11).

These Scripture passages confirm that Jesus Christ has full authority over the creation and that His authority extends over all the evil authorities on earth including fallen angels; even Satan has no power over Him. (John 14:30 NKJV) "*I will no longer talk much with you, for the ruler of this world is coming, and he has nothing in Me.*" In other words, Jesus said that Satan has no power over Him, has no claim on Him, has no right over Him as all authority has been given to Him by God. In fact, the Father has given all things, including Satan, into Jesus' hands:

"The Father loves the Son, and has given all things into His hand." (John 3:35) (NKJV). *"He also has authority to judge all men 'For the Father judges no one, but has committed all judgment to the Son, that all should honour the Son just as they honour the Father. He who does not honour the Son does not honour the Father who sent Him.'"* (John 5:22-23 NKJV).

Likewise, He has the authority to raise people from the dead and give eternal life to those who are righteous believers (John 17:1-3, John 6:40, John 10:28, John 11:25-26).

Jesus demonstrated His authority and powers in diverse ways and these are few of them in the following table:

How Jesus Demonstrated His Authority

He forgives sins (Mark 2:10), heals the paralyzed (Luke 5:17-23)	He has authority in teaching (Mark 1:21-22), He teaches with authority (Luke 4:31-32)
He heals every sickness and every disease (Matt. 9:35)	He rebukes and casts out demons (Matt. 17.18, Luke 9.42)
He has authority over nature by calming the wind and the sea (Mark 4.39)	He has authority to take action when appropriate (John 2:13-18).

He has authority to cast out demons (Mark 7:29-30)	He has power to deliver people from infirmities, from oppression and loose people from the Satanic bondage (Luke 13:10-17)
He has authority to heal all kinds of impediments, blindness, deafness, and authority to release people from demonic attacks (Matt. 12:22)	He raises the dead (Luke 7:12-15, John 11:41-45)

The authority that Jesus Christ gives us has the same effect and the same impact the way Jesus demonstrated it. He raises the dead; we too can raise the dead. He heals all manner of sicknesses and diseases; we should be able to do the same. He casts out demons; we should be able to cast out demons. Finally, Jesus told us that we can do greater works – meaning, we can do greater miracles (John 14:12).

Also, as we read from the parable of the talents in Chapter 13, and likewise in the parable of the ten Minas (Luke 19:11-28), and as workers in the Vineyard (Matt. 20:1-16) that we are created to take responsibilities on earth, manage things that are under our care and to take good care of them and utilise them wisely to the best of our ability.

We also read in Gal. 3:26-29:

"For you are all sons of God through faith in Christ Jesus. For as many of you as were baptized into Christ have put on Christ. There is neither Jew nor Greek, there is neither slave nor free, there is neither male nor female; for you are all one in Christ Jesus. And if you are Christ's, then you are Abraham's seed, and heirs according to the promise."

Since we are God's heirs: *"Therefore you are no longer a slave but a son, and if a son, then an heir of God through Christ."* (Gal. 4:7 NKJV). And heirs are recipients of divine promise (Gal. 3:29) and such receive allotted possessions by the right of sonship. Likewise, in the Book of Romans:

"...and if children, then heirs—heirs of God and joint heirs with Christ, if indeed we suffer with Him, that we may also be glorified together." (Rom. 8:17 NKJV).

We are not only heirs but also joint heirs with Christ, meaning all that belongs to Jesus as the firstborn also belongs to us. So, as joint heirs with Christ and as His representatives or stewards on earth we have the right to exercise power over the enemy in Jesus' name. And as His ambassadors – His stewards and representatives of the Heavenly Kingdom on earth, we have His authority throughout the earth (Matt. 28:18-20, Matt. 16:19, 18:18-19, 2 Cor. 5:20).

The next chapter expounds further on the steward-master relationship and what it entails.

Chapter 13
Co-Workers

"For we are God's fellow workers; you are God's field, you are God's building." (1 Cor. 3:9 NKJV).

With this concept of stewardship as explained vividly by Paul, we are able to view accurately and correctly and to value not only our possessions, but more importantly, human life also. In essence, stewardship defines our purpose on earth as assigned to us by God Himself. It is our divinely-given opportunity to join with God in His universal and eternal redemptive programme (Matthew 28:19-20). Stewardship is not God taking something from us: it is His way of imparting His richest gifts to us, His people.

Further understanding of how the final account of our stewardship on earth will be played out on the Judgment Day is explained in Matt. 25:14-33:

The Scriptures above dwell on the day of reckoning, a day where each of us must give an account of our stewardship on earth. The first steward had five talents and manages the master's affairs well and makes profits, likewise the second steward. But the third decides to hide his talent in the hope that he can justify himself.

This is one of Jesus' most significant parables regarding work and it is set in the context of investments. A rich man delegates the management of his wealth to his servants, much as investors in today's markets do. He gives five talents, a large unit of money to the first servant, two talents to the second and one talent to the third. Two of the servants earn a hundred percent return by trading with the funds, but the third servant hides the money in the ground and earns nothing. The rich man returns, rewards the two who made money but severely punishes the servant who did nothing.

The meaning of the parable extends far beyond financial investments. God has given each of us a wide variety of gifts and He expects us to employ those gifts in His service. It is not acceptable merely to put those gifts on hold, not to use them or ignore them. Like the three servants, we do not have gifts of the same degree. The return God expects of us is commensurate with the gifts we have been given. The servant who received one talent was not condemned for failing to reach the five-talent goal; he was condemned because he did nothing with what he was given. The gifts we receive from God include skills, abilities, connections, positions, education, experiences, special knowledge, creativity, intelligence, technical know-how and much more. The point of the parable is that we are to use whatever we have been given for God's purposes and glory. The severe consequences to the unproductive servant, far beyond anything caused by laziness, wrong attitudes, precipitous foolish decisions, tell us that we are to invest our lives, not waste them.

Yet the particular talent invested in the parable is money, on the order of a million U.S. dollars in today's world, as some researchers claim. In this 21st century, this imperative point is obscured because the word "talent" has come to refer mainly to skills or abilities. It depicts investing our skills and abilities in whatever right and good things we are passionate about to accomplish godly purposes in a godly manner. In the end, the master praises the two trustworthy servants with the words, "Well done, good and trustworthy servants (Matthew 25:23). In these words, we see that the master cares about the results "well done", the methods "good", and the motivation "trustworthy" and there is a reward, "Enter into the joy of your Lord" – enjoyment on earth and in Heaven.

It is vital to understand that business or individual growth, progress, success, entrepreneurships, manufacturing or provision of good and services and much more are good ways to demonstrate the fulfilment of our skills and abilities, talents, which in return advances and help others. We should invest our skills and abilities, but also our wealth and the resources made available to us at work and wherever we may find ourselves, all for the business of God's kingdom. This includes the provision of houses for the needy, the homeless and the poor, the manufacturing of needed goods and services. The individual who teaches the word of God is fulfilling this parable. The volunteer who helps out to save lives as medical doctor, nurse, carer or other health practitioner is also fulfilling this parable. So is the entrepreneur who starts a new business and gives jobs to others; those who build schools or hospitals to meet the needs of people; the health service practitioner who initiates an AIDS-awareness campaign, cancer research, diabetes, Alzheimer's', and dementia support groups to help those in such situation; the car manufacturer who develops transport systems that can help us foster the gospel across the world, and the makers of aeroplanes which can connect us to the rest of the world and much more.

It is imperative to understand that God does not endow people with matching or necessarily similar gifts. If we do as well as we can with the gifts given to us by God, we will receive His "Well done.", a good outcome of the rightful use of the talents made available to us. Although the gifts do not have equal worth people do. At the same time, the parable ends with the talent taken from the third servant and being given to the first servant with ten talents making it now eleven talents. Equal worth does not necessarily mean equal reward. Some positions in life require more skill or ability than another and are rewarded accordingly. The two good productive servants who did excellently are rewarded in different amounts and they are both commended equally with good rewards on earth and also with the opportunity to spend the rest of their lives in Heaven. The parable enlightens and gave us more insights as to why we must always use whatever talents we have been given to the best of our ability for God's honour and glory. When we have done that, we are on an equal playing field with other fruitful, faithful, trustworthy servants of God. So, whatever talent God entrusted to us for the purpose for which we are created on earth, it is good to use it to honour God and for His glory.

Chapter 14

The only Way to Heaven – Jesus Christ

"*Jesus said to him, 'I am the way, the truth, and the life. No one comes to the Father except through Me.'*" (John 14:6 NKJV)

We must first of all settle this in our minds that God exists and He is our creator (Gen. 1:1). And we must also resolve in our minds that Christianity is true and the Kingdom of God is also true and that Jesus Christ died on the cross, shed His blood to redeem us by offering forgiveness of our sins through His blood (Matt. 26:28, Mark 1:15, 10:15, Acts 2:38, 13:38, Col. 1:13-15); and that Jesus Christ rose from death (Luke 24:1-8, Rom. 6:9-10, John 11:24-25, 1 Thess. 4:14) and made eternal life available to us.

For anyone who is not yet convinced that Jesus Christ, Our Lord and Saviour, is the only way to Heaven, the question of knowing our eternal location when our time is up on earth may look confusing. The question whether we should put our faith in Jesus Christ is another important aspect but making this issue our priority is the best option.

There are three important questions that many would like to have answers to such as:

- Who are the people who will be saved or rescued from eternal punishment?
- Is Jesus Christ the only way to Heaven?
- Will those who have not heard the gospel be saved? See Appendix B.

The first two questions will be addressed in this chapter, but of first importance is to establish the answers to these aforementioned questions through the word of God. In the Gospel of John:

"Jesus said to him, 'I am the way, the truth, and the life. No one comes to the Father except through Me.'" (John 14:6 NKJV).

These words of Jesus explicitly state that the only way to the Father in Heaven (John 10:7, John 14:6, John 11:25) is through Him – Jesus Christ and by doing the will of the Heavenly Father (Matt. 7:21).

Do understand that everything about Jesus' purpose on earth is about Redemption – saving us from our sins, healing us, protecting us and delivering us from Satan and much more. But the ultimate goal is for us to gain eternal life – to make it to Heaven. The name "Jesus" means "Jehovah saves"; the word "salvation" means to "rescue". Jesus' name describes His mission and purpose of coming to earth. He is the Way, the Truth and the Life. He gives us the way to build our relationship with God and to be united with Him.

You can read more on why Jesus Christ came in appendix A.

In order to answer the first and second questions:

- Who are the people that will be saved or rescued from eternal punishment?
- Is Jesus Christ the only way to Heaven?

The Scriptures (John 3:3-7, John 3:16-18, Eph. 2:8) makes it crystal clear that to be saved or rescued from eternal punishment or to avoid going to Hell, we must be born again – believe in Jesus Christ as Lord and Saviour who died and shed His blood on the cross of Calvary, who paid for all our sins through His blood and we receive redemption through His blood (Eph. 1:7, Rom. 5:8-9). We are saved and with the help of the Holy Spirit at work in our lives, we obey Him and walk by the Spirit of God and do all that He says, being word practitioners, hearers and doers of the word of God (James 1:25, Ps. 1:1-3).

"He who believes and is baptized will be saved; but he who does not believe will be condemned." (Mark 16:16 NKJV).

And with the second question – Is Jesus Christ the only way to Heaven?

This is made clear in John 14:6 as well as in Acts 4:12.

"Jesus said to him, 'I am the way, the truth, and the life. No one comes to the Father except through Me.' "(John 14:6 NKJV).

"Nor is there salvation in any other, for there is no other name under heaven given among men by which we must be saved." (Acts 4:12 NKJV).

All these Scripture passages point to the fact that there is no other way and no other religion that can lead us to Heaven except through Jesus Christ – Christianity. Other questions to ask are "Why is it that people can be saved only through Jesus Christ alone? Am I not able to save myself?

First however, let us answer them in stages and these are the answers:

1. **We cannot save ourselves:**

"As it is written: 'There is none righteous, no, not one; There is none who understands; There is none who seeks after God. They have all turned aside; They have together become unprofitable; There is none who does good, no, not one." "Their throat is an open tomb; With their tongues they have practiced deceit"; "The poison of asps is under their lips'; "Whose mouth is full of cursing and bitterness." "Their feet are swift to shed blood; Destruction and misery are in their ways; and the way of peace they have not known." "There is no fear of God before their eyes." "Now we know that whatever the law says, it says to those who are under the law, that every mouth may be stopped, and all the world may become guilty before God. Therefore, by the deeds of the law no flesh will be justified in His sight, for by the law is the knowledge of sin." (Romans 3:10-20 NKJV).

2. **We cannot make ourselves good enough for God or make ourselves right with God on our own:**

Based on what we do, the law does not give us a way to justify ourselves or to be considered right in God's sight; instead it tells us what sin is and how to live above it and this is what Paul was explicitly emphasising in Romans:

"Therefore by the deeds of the law no flesh will be justified in His sight, for by the law is the knowledge of sin." (Rom. 3:20 NKJV).

So, good works alone will not get us to Heaven; we need the help of Jesus Christ. Unfortunately, none of us can save ourselves; none of us can succeed without Christ's help (Rom. 3:23-26, John 14:6).

If we know Christ intimately, we will still continue to do good works (Gal. 6:8-10) but our relationship with God should not be the result of the good works but rather the result of God's gracious acceptance of us because of what Jesus did (Eph. 2:8-10).

So, if we cannot save ourselves and other people too cannot save themselves by their works or by the good deeds or charity works they have done on earth, no one else or no other religion can save us except Jesus Christ, Our Saviour.

3. **Jesus Christ was sent from Heaven to earth to save us:** (John 3:16 NKJV)

Jesus is the only Saviour of the whole world. He died and rose again to make atonement for our sins and brought reconciliation to the world, redemption and justification for all (John 1:29, John 4:42, Romans 5:17-18, 2 Cor.5:18-20, Col. 1:19-23, 1 John 2:2, 1 John 4:14-19). So, with all due respect to other religions, God has chosen only this way to save people in the world – through Jesus Christ Our Saviour (John 14:6, Acts 4:12).

Jesus Christ died to provide an atoning sacrifice sufficient to cover every sin of every person. The blood of Jesus that was shed on the Cross of Calvary was enough to pay for the sins of all the human race. So, there is no limit to the saving grace of redemptive blood of Christ. And to be saved, we must respond to God's grace (Eph. 2:8-9).

The answer to the first question, "Who are the people that will be saved or who are the ones that may go to Hell?" is found here: John 3:16, 18:

"God loves the whole world... whoever believes should not perish but have everlasting life" but verse 18 adds *"He who believes in Him is not condemned; but he who does not believe is condemned already, because he has not believed in the name of the only begotten Son of God."*

Whoever believes in Jesus Christ Our Lord and Saviour who died and rose again, who shed His blood for the remission of our sins and whoever walks according to His precepts will not go to Hell but rather have eternal life and also have the opportunity of living with the Heavenly Father in Heaven. However, those who do not believe in Him are condemned already – meaning they will end up in Hell.

Our Heavenly Father desires all people to be saved and to come to the knowledge of the truth. (1 Tim 2:4, 2 Peter 3:9). He does not want anyone to perish, but for all to come to repentance, (1 Tim 4:10). God is the Saviour of all people, especially of those who believe. What does it mean to believe?

In the Gospel of John 3:3-7, the prerequisite of entering into Heaven is to be born again, to be baptised in water, to be Spirit filled – filled with the Holy Spirit and, of course, to live the Christ-like life, doing the will of the Heavenly Father (Matt. 6:33, Matt. 12:50, Gal. 5:16-26, Eph. 4:31-32, Phil. 2:2, Phil. 4:8-9, Col. 3:5, 1 Thess. 4:3, James 1:22-27, 1 Peter 2:15, 1 John 1:8-9). And those who refuse to accept the Lord Jesus Christ as their Lord and Saviour shall be condemned – end up in eternal death – Hell – (Matt. 10:33, John 3:18, Rev. 20:15).

If you have decided to give your life to Jesus' Christ, please pray this simple prayer:

"Lord Jesus, I acknowledge my sins and I confess them before you today (confess each ...) forgive me all my sins and let my heart be cleansed by your blood, my Saviour who died on the cross of Calvary and rose again the third day. Show me your mercy today and I invite you, Jesus Christ, into my life. I also invite the Holy Spirit to come into my life to stay. I will allow the Holy Spirit to lead me daily, guide me, counsel me. Teach me your words and your ways of living. Teach me your way of righteousness and holiness and help me to live in the light of faith and to walk in obedience to your will. Oh Lord always in Jesus' name. Amen."

Please find a Bible-based church around you to attend and be a part of that community in order to continue to engage in Kingdom works (Heb. 10:25 NKJV). This will be a place where you can be mentored and thus grow in your relationship with God (Prov. 27:17).

Chapter 15
Preparing For Our Eternal Home

"For we must all appear before the judgment seat of Christ, that each one may receive the things done in the body, according to what he has done, whether good or bad." (2 Cor. 5:10 NKJV).

Our acceptance of Jesus Christ as our Lord and Saviour will determine our eternal location (John 3:16).

The questions to you are: What have you been doing with your life? What have you been doing with your talent and the personal assignment that God created you for here on earth? What did you use the time on earth to achieve? These and many more are what we will be accountable for. Read more in Appendix C.

Why are we then responsible for how we spent our lives on earth? Here are the reasons in the first chapter of Genesis and in the Gospel of Luke with reference to the parable illustrated by Jesus Christ:

"So he called ten of his servants, delivered to them ten minas, and said to them, 'Do business till I come.'" (Luke 19:13 NKJV).

In other words, we are to use our lives to give glory to God on earth, engage in the expansion of the Kingdom of God, winning souls for Christ Jesus and much more.

"In the beginning God created the heavens and the earth. The earth was without form, and void; and darkness was on the face of the deep. And the Spirit of God was hovering over the face of the waters." (Gen. 1:1-2 NKJV).

"... Then God said, 'Let Us make man in Our image, according to Our likeness; let them have dominion over the fish of the sea, over the birds of the air, and over the cattle, over all the earth and over every creeping thing that creeps on the earth.' So God created man in His own image; in the image of God He created him; male and female He created them. Then God blessed them, and God said to them, 'Be fruitful and multiply; fill the earth and subdue it; have dominion over the fish of the sea, over the birds of the air, and over every living thing that moves on the earth.'" (Gen. 1:26-28 NKJV).

It all goes back to the time of the creation and why God our creator created us in the first place and why He gave us the earth to rule and to dominate, to be productive, to subdue, to conquer, to replenish and to develop it. As the creator (Gen. 1:1), He has absolute rights of ownership over all things in Heaven and on earth (Ps. 146:6). And anyone who is given the responsibility of managing a place, an estate or a business, etc., is called a "steward". In the dictionary a steward is defined as "A person whose responsibility it is to take care of something, a person employed to manage another's property, especially a large house or estate, financial affairs, etc. or responsible for overseeing and for the protection of something considered worth caring for and preserving". What does the Bible mean when it calls believers "stewards"? Also see Chapter 13.

"The earth is the Lord's, and all its fullness, The world and those who dwell therein." (Ps. 24:1 NKJV).

"He was in the beginning with God. All things were made through Him, and without Him nothing was made that was made." (John 1:2-3 NKJV).

First of all, it is clear that God is the owner of everything – living and non-living things, including our lives. The second important thing that we must recognise is that God created all resources that we can find on earth for our good use (Gen. 1:26, Matt. 28:18, John 1:3-4).

And the third important thing is that God created us for a purpose (Jer. 1:5, Matt. 28:18-20, Acts 26:16-18).

These are the three imperatives that we must be aware of and that sum up the purpose of existence on this earth: First, God created everything and that includes the human race; second, God provided the resources that humanity needs and third, God gave each human being responsibilities to carry out on earth. So, what have we been doing with the opportunities that we have been given? Do remember that one day we have to give an account of our responsibilities on earth. Read more in Appendix C.

Now we know that God owns everything in Heaven and on earth, and that He gave us the opportunity and responsibility of managing what He owns as His stewards. At some point in life and in the life beyond we are expected to give an account to God of how we managed what He gave us. So, Biblical stewardship is about identifying and recognising that God's resources are to be managed wisely and for the expansion of His Kingdom.

Do understand that relationship is another exciting and important aspect of our lives. Relationships – our relationships with friends, parents, husband or wife, siblings, children, grandchildren, school friends and work colleagues. Likewise, there is the steward-master relationship and this involves two people – a master who hands over His resources to the steward who shall ask for accounting one day and a steward who is entrusted to manage the resources of His master and who must account for how they were utilised and invested.

Friends, we are stewards and we are accountable to God for all that we do on earth. So, what have you been doing with the life and the personal assignments God made available to you from the time you know right from wrong? Are you using His resources wisely? Are you using your time, God's resources and all that you have to promote God's Kingdom, winning souls or are you are using it to glorify the devil? Ponder on your way of life, your decisions, your choices: are they rightful? And do you think God can be proud of you as a good steward or otherwise? The good news is that it is not too late to make amends and begin to live a new life.

In preparing for the eternal home, in this case Heaven if you have fulfilled the prerequisites as expounded in Chapter 14, you now need to continue doing His will. You need to come to terms with your sin not by making promises to God that you end up not fulfilling, nor by saying, "From now on I will change, I will be better, I still have time". But it can only be by confirming that Jesus Christ is the only way to Heaven (John 14:6). And not only that, but also confessing all your sins, then accepting Jesus

109

Christ as your Lord and Saviour, who died on the cross, paid your debt by the shedding of His blood. Then, your sin will be forgiven. There is no other way, there is no other person and there is no other name by which we can be saved. The only way is through Jesus Christ (Acts 4:12), who died, shed His blood to pay for our sin-debt and rose again so that we can have eternal life and for us to be where He is – In Heaven with the Heavenly Father (John 14:1-3). And if you have not put your trust in Jesus Christ, do it now. Be sure that Heaven will be your eternal Home.

Chapter 16
Keys to Keeping Eternity in Mind

"Not everyone who says to Me, 'Lord, Lord,' shall enter the kingdom of heaven, but he who does the will of My Father in heaven. Many will say to Me in that day, 'Lord, Lord, have we not prophesied in Your name, cast out demons in Your name, and done many wonders in Your name?' And then I will declare to them, 'I never knew you; depart from Me, you who practice lawlessness!'" (Matt. 7:21-23 NKJV)

We learnt in the previous chapters about securing our eternal residence – Heaven. There are prerequisites that must be adhered to in order to have eternal life and I will call these the keys required to enter the right side of eternity. In order words, what are the prerequisites of securing the right side of eternity – Heaven? They are:

- **You must be saved: Be Born Again:** *"Jesus answered and said to him, 'Most assuredly, I say to you, unless one is born again, he cannot see the kingdom of God.'"* (John 3:3 NKJV). You must receive Jesus Christ as your personal Lord and Saviour (John 3:16-17 NKJV).

If you were to die today and stand before God and He asked, 'Why should I allow you into Heaven?' what would you say? Are you qualified? Do you think the life you live on earth qualifies you for the right side of eternity – Heaven?

So, have you been thinking and planning right now on earth where you would be going or would like to be after your journey is completed on earth? Have you been preparing and planning for life after death? And if one falls short of the glory, there are no make-up plans or emergency plans to re-apply or to change your lifestyle. Life in eternity is permanent; there is no change of mind or change of position and, at that time, you no longer have control over your life and decisions.

- **It also requires knowing God personally (Phil. 3:10):** being saved through grace by faith (Eph. 2:8), doing the will of the Heavenly Father (Matt. 7:21); living in peace will all people and holiness (Heb. 12:14) and being filled with the Holy Spirit and being led by the Holy Spirit (John 14:26, John 16: 13, Rom. 8:14, Gal. 5:16-18, 25).

In this context, Jesus related a story of a lawyer who was self-righteous and wanted to put Jesus to the test (Luke 10:25). He asked what he must do to gain eternal life and Jesus answered with the requirements of keeping the commandments. If you can keep all of the commandments, it would seem that you could enter eternal life. However, nobody can keep all of the commandments. Therefore, Jesus' comments to this man show that justification can only be through faith since no one can keep all of the commandments. This is why in Eph. 2:8 we read that we are saved by grace through faith. Also, Romans 3:20, 28 and Galatians 2:16 tell us that no one is justified in the sight of God by the law but by faith in Jesus Christ and not by the works of the law.

The Law cannot save us because we are incapable of fully keeping it (Matt. 19:16-21). Therefore, salvation is by grace through faith.

- **It requires living a sin-free life with the help of the Holy Spirit (Gal. 5:19-21, Gal. 5:25-26, Eph. 5:1-7, 8-20):** Some have answered and said, "I am a good person and I have never hurt anyone" but these answers would not get you into Heaven. God's forgiveness our sins is also required so that we are truly reconciled to Him (1 John 1:8-9, Rom. 8:1, 2 Cor. 13:5). Also by helping the poor, serving Him and doing His will (Matt. 19:21-22).
- **Living the Christ-like life on earth:** In Eph. 5:1-2, John 17:3, 2 Peter 3:18, this is an ongoing process as we demonstrate positive change in the way we live, growing to know God and building our relationship with Him (Phil. 3:10). And it is a continuous process of strengthening a Christ-centred life through the help of the Holy Spirit with grace to be like Him.

The following passages support these ideas (Rom. 12:2, Col. 3:5-10, James 4:11-12, Rom. 12:17-21, 1 John 2:15-17, Phil. 4:8-9).

- **Seeking the Kingdom of God First:** (Matt. 6:33). Always making God and His Kingdom your priority on a daily basis. To do that, we must always represent rightfully and honour the

Kingdom of God by the way we deal with: work, family, friends, goals, leisure, colleagues, money, people, academics, pleasure, desires, interests, relationships and much more. As we live our lives any of these can unknowingly be allowed to move or shift God out of the first place, if we do not purposely choose to give Him first place in every area of our lives? Now the question is, "What is most important to you in life? What is your priority? Is it the challenges that you face, problems, difficulties or issues of life or what is going on in the world? Why can't you just yield and obey Jesus' instruction today and make Him the first importance, the priority in your life and see the difference He makes in your life? And when you make Him your priority, the first importance in all areas of your life and live right (righteousness describes the rightfulness of Jesus Christ, He is always right and will never be wrong, He lives right, He speaks right, He dresses right, He relates to people right, acts right and much more), Jesus promised that God will give all you need daily if you live for Him: sound health, divine protection and divine guidance; breakthroughs (marital, relationship, career, financial, academics, etc.), abundant life, exemption from evil, setbacks, misfortune and tragedies.

- **Only those who do the will of the Heavenly Father:** *"Not everyone who says to Me, 'Lord, Lord,' shall enter the kingdom of heaven, but he who does the will of My Father in heaven."* (Matt. 7:21 NKJV).

And here is one of the main points – those who DO the Father's Will. We must be doers of the word of God; we must be Bible practitioners, doing what the Bible says (James 1:25, Ps 1:1-3).

The Bible is the word of God, the mind of God, God Himself – active and alive – (Heb. 4:12). James emphasises that it is those who are the doers of the word and doers of the work that will be blessed in whatever they do (James 1:25).

Chapter 17
Heaven is a Place for You

"But there shall by no means enter it anything that defiles, or causes an abomination or a lie, but only those who are written in the Lamb's Book of Life." (Rev. 21:27 NKJV).

Now, it is very clear that the destination of believers in Christ is HEAVEN – "to be present with the Lord" at the end of our time on earth:

"We are confident, yes, well pleased rather to be absent from the body and to be present with the Lord." (2 Cor. 5:8 NKJV).

"For I am hard-pressed between the two, having a desire to depart and be with Christ, which is far better." (Phil. 1:23 NKJV).

Heaven is prepared for all who have received Christ Jesus as their Lord and Saviour by faith (John 14:2-3), those who love the Lord and obey His commandments (Rev. 22:12-14). It is a pure place (Rev. 21:1-2, 27). It is important to understand that Heaven is a pure and holy place just as God is Holy (1 Peter 1:16, Heb. 12:14). He cannot allow anything unholy into Heaven otherwise it would not be Heaven anymore, just as an author wrote, "If

Heaven is not a perfect place, it will just be like a re-run of earth, but up there!". But the Heavenly Father is perfect: *"Therefore you shall be perfect, just as your Father in heaven is perfect."* (Matt. 5:48 NKJV). Since our Heavenly Father is perfect and Heaven is a perfect place, how can people who are not perfect go and live with a perfect Father in a perfect place – Heaven? But thanks be to Jesus Christ our Lord and Saviour who came from Heaven to redeem us from all our sins. And through Jesus Christ's death, His atoning blood and through His resurrection if we received Him in our life as our Lord and Saviour and live according to His will and ways – Christ-like life, we are now made right with God and can receive His perfect life through the Holy Spirit. We can gain eternal life and we have the opportunity to live in Heaven with a holy and perfect Father.

Heaven

In My Father's house are many mansions; if it were not so, I would have told you. I go to prepare a place for you. And if I go and prepare a place for you, I will come again and receive you to Myself; that where I am, there you may be also. (John 14:2-3)

One of our greatest joys as a redeemed child of God should be longing for our eternal home – our Heavenly Home. Jesus described it this way, "In *My Father's house are many mansions, if it were not so, I would have told you. I go to prepare a place for you...*" We should always remind ourselves that we are only here just as sojourners – passing through. Our destination is Heaven. That is why we should always live with Heaven in mind, keeping eternity in our heart as we live.

And for you to be preparing and getting ready on a daily basis, always set your mind on the things that are above, on the reality of Heaven and not on things on earth, avoid things that will cause you to miss Heaven (Col. 3:1-10, Matt. 6:33). Then, allow the Christ-like life to grow, to be manifest every day of your life and in every situation that you may find yourself. Always show mercy to people, be kind, be humble, be patient, always forgiving. If you have a complaint against another, just as Christ forgave you, do forgive the individual. Do not keep grudges, do not gossip, do not backbite. Do not be involved in false accusations against another. Bear with one another; let the agape love of Christ prevail about all things. Embrace unity, peace and holiness at all costs in your life and be thankful at all times. Finally, let the word of Christ dwell in you always (Col. 3:12-17, Matt. 6:33).

There is no place like Heaven. It is the best place to be at the end of our journey on earth (1 Cor. 2:9, Heb. 11:16, Rev. 21:4, 12-27, Rev. 22:1-5, Mat. 6:19-21, John 3:16)

In whatever you do or engage in on earth, do all for the glory of God. Keep living with Heaven in Mind.

Chapter 18

What is Your Decision? What Choice Have You Made – Heaven or Hell?

If you were to be asked these questions while you are still living, what would your response be to them?

1. Can you answer these questions?

Have you ever lied once? Have you ever disobeyed, rebelled, deceived, manipulated, cheated, misled people, bullied, abused, accused people wrongfully, persecuted, hated, once – just once? Let's be honest and truthful, we have all done one or two of these. With such we have become unholy, impure and no unholy person can enter Heaven. But thanks be to Jesus Christ who came to redeem us from lawless deeds and from all wickedness – He purifies us for Himself His own chosen and very special people to be His own possession and to be enthusiastic for doing what is good:

"Who gave Himself for us, that He might redeem us from every lawless deed and purify for Himself His own special people, zealous for good works." (Titus 2:14 NKJV).

Likewise, do you know anyone who has never sinned before? Do you know anyone who has never broken any of God's laws? The answer is surely "no". Hence, that is why Jesus Christ came, died and paid for all our sins through His blood as He rose again to make eternal life available to those who received Him as their personal Lord and Saviour (John 1:12, John 3:16). Then, we can now be saved by living the Christ-like life continuously and to be like Christ. To be holy and righteous like Him, doing His will, we can now meet the prerequisite of gaining access into Heaven.

2. Why does a loving Heavenly Father create a place like Hell and allow some people to go there?

Here on earth, there are rules and regulations to abide by. The same applies in the Kingdom of God. Let me give you an example: if someone you love was unjustly killed and the murderer was caught, confessed and was found guilty by the jury and to everyone's amazement, the judge says, "I release him free with no charge", how would you feel? Could you believe that? Would you be upset with such judgment? Would you think that's fair? You already know that when anyone breaks the law and confesses to it, there must be punishment. Otherwise, there is no fairness; there is no justice. With this deep thought, you can better understand that Hell involves justice and is not a hate issue.

To further understand why Hell is created: have you ever been bitter towards anyone? Or talked negatively behind the back of someone or gossiped about someone? The truth is that most people would find that unpleasant or toxic. So, their anger might turn into bitterness and bitterness to hatred. And that alone makes the person guilty of bitterness and unwilling to forgive. That, too, is a sin. But the following Scripture passages offer ways to live above such (Prov. 20:22, Matt. 6:14-15, Rom. 12:17-21, Eph. 4:31-32, Heb. 12:14-15).

It is also important to note that God does not send anyone to Hell: they made such choice by rejecting Jesus Christ, the Saviour (John 3:16-21). In other words, they send themselves to Hell through their wrong choices – with their own sovereign will power. Hence, human beings must make a choice while on earth as to where he or she would like to spend eternity: Heaven or Hell?

3. Have you ever hated anyone?

Have you ever felt displeased or felt intense dislike towards someone? Such makes us guilty of hatred. In earthly law, killing someone is considered as murder but in the Kingdom of God, simply hating another person is considered murder:

"Whoever hates his brother is a murderer, and you know that no murderer has eternal life abiding in him." (1 John 3:15 NKJV).

This Scripture passage makes it clear that no murderer will enter eternal life – will not enter Heaven.

4. Have you ever lied?

If the answer is "no", then you are probably telling another lie. The truth is we have all lied at some point in our lives either in our early years before we know Christ or before we received the Holy Spirit. At that time when we did not know God, we would have been guilty of being a liar, but if anyone is still engaging in lying, this is a sin and no sinner will be allowed in to Heaven.

The list goes on and on but the good news is that through redemption if we accept Jesus Christ into our lives as our personal Lord and Saviour and be willing to live a continuous Christ-like life, walking by the Holy Spirit, if we live a holy life and obey Him, then our Heavenly home will be guaranteed. This is one of the reasons why Jesus came:

- **He came to save sinners and the lost:** (Matt. 18:11, Luke 19:10, 1 Tim. 1:15)
- **He came to put away sin:** (John 1:29, 1 John 3:5)
- **He came to bear our sin:** (Heb. 9:28, 1 Peter 2:24)
- **He came to provide a pattern of holy living and a Christ-like lifestyle for us to follow:** (Matt. 11:29, 1 Peter 1:15-16)
- **He came to destroy the works of the devil:** (1 John 3:8, Heb. 2:14)
- **He came to reveal the Father:** (John 14:9-10) and much more.

Have you ever asked yourself; What have you done with all the opportunities that God has given you on earth? What are you here for? Who are you living for? Apostle Paul described his own purpose of living this way:

"*… according to my earnest expectation and hope that in nothing I shall be ashamed, but with all boldness, as always, so now also Christ will be magnified in my body, whether by life or by death. For to me, to live is Christ, and to die is gain.*" (Phil. 1:20-21 NKJV).

He chose to live for Christ. He understood the essence of living for Christ and he determined to live for Him till the end; Peter too left all to follow Jesus (Matt. 19:27, Mark 10:28, Luke 18:28). So, who are you living for or following today? Christ or people or social media, or celebrities? Things of this world that will fade away, trends of fashion, technologies? Are you idolising a human being? Some of these things may not be wrong if used positively?

Paul, Peter, other men and women did make up their minds to live for Jesus without holding back. Why are you holding back your life? Your life is supposed to be used for the advancement of the universal redemptive programme of God, winning souls and evangelising for the Kingdom of God. You are meant to invest your life and time for the eternal Gospel – Gospel of Christ.

What about the certainty of Christ's return, the reality of eternity (Heaven or Hell), future resurrection, Rapture, Judgement? Do they not have any impact, any effect on your life? Remember that a day of accounting of what you have done in the body will come (2 Cor. 5:10, Rom. 14:12). There is no salvation after death, no more repentance, no more mercy after death, no second chance. Let us ponder for a moment. Are you ready to have your work judged? Have you been faithful living for Christ, obeying His instructions, doing His will and witnessing for Him? What if Christ should come today, where would you be placed – Heaven or Hell? What if Christ should return any moment from now or today or tomorrow or even before you finish reading this book? You should now take your decisions and life seriously or as a matter of urgency start living with a view to be prepared always just like the five wise virgins (Matt. 25:1-13). Jesus can return any day, at any hour, seize each opportunity that you have as if it is the last opportunity. Do not stay idle, be occupied till He comes (Luke 19:13). Keep growing in God. Build your relationship with Him, witnessing for Him, praying for people, healing the sick, raising the dead, curing diseases, casting out demons and much more till He comes (Matt. 10:7-8, 10:1,8, Luke 9:1, 10:9).

And likewise our Heavenly Father desires for us to be more like Him (Rom. 12:1-2, Eph. 4:14-16), 2 Peter 3:17-18), to be His imitators (Eph. 5:1), to be an example to believers in word, in conduct, in love, in spirit, in faith and in purity (1 Tim. 4:12).

Chapter 19
The Ways God Has Got Through to Us. We Must Not Miss the Opportunity

God's love for us is unconditional and that is why He sent His Only Son to redeem us from eternal death so that we can receive eternal life:

"And this is eternal life, that they may know You, the only true God, and Jesus Christ whom You have sent." (John 17:3 NKJV).

We have no excuse at all why we should not go to Heaven. These are some of the facts:

- ✓ Our Heavenly Father created the heavens and the earth, nature and the things we can see around us. These form the evidence that God exists (Gen. 1:1-2).
- ✓ Jesus came to earth and died for us and paid the debt of our sins (Rom. 3:24-26, Heb. 10:12).
- ✓ He offers to us free salvation by grace through faith (John 3:16, Eph. 2:8).
- ✓ He provides ways to know Him and grow in Him (John 14:6, John 17:3).

- ✓ We are given the ability to differentiate what is right from what is wrong – conscience.
- ✓ We have churches (Christ-centred churches) around us for us to know God.
- ✓ Someone may have preached to us in school, college, university, on the train, car, on ships or cruise, at workplace or airport or in a city.
- ✓ Someone may have given us a Bible or tracts or Christian articles.
- ✓ Jesus died and rose again to prepare a place for us in Heaven (John 14:1-2). That is why He was sent. We must keep eternity in mind and also fulfil His Kingdom purpose.
- ✓ This book is written for us to gain deep knowledge about eternal life, why we must not miss the opportunity that Jesus Christ makes available to us. It contains the keys to living a Christ-like life on earth and to be able to make accurate and correct decisions right here on earth regarding our eternal home – Heaven to meet our Heavenly Father.

Our ultimate goal is to get to Heaven after we leave the earth.

If you died today, where would you go? Heaven or Hell. The choice is yours based on the decisions, choices you make on earth. Do remember that after death it is impossible to repent, there is no salvation after death, no change of choice; you cannot change your mind, and neither do you have the power to change your location. As I have explained in Chapter 4, eternity means permanence: a state where no human has authority to make changes to their decisions or choices already made.

Is there any reason why you should not turn to Jesus Christ right now? Is there any reason why you cannot surrender your life to Jesus Christ today? If you would like to, please say this prayer:

"Dear Jesus Christ, I thank you for dying on the cross of Calvary for me, thank you for making salvation available to me freely by grace through faith. And I am sorry for all the things that I have done wrong, I confess all my sins, ask for forgiveness of all my sins and if there are things that I may have done wrong unknown to me or if there are things that I may have done wrong to other people, Father, in the name of Jesus Christ, forgive me and please let your mercy prevail over your judgement. From today, I decide to live the Christ-like life, the life that pleases, honours and give glory to you at all times in Jesus Christ's name. I invite you into my life as my personal Lord and Saviour from today, and I also invite the Holy Spirit to come into my life to teach me your way of peace and holiness from today in Jesus Christ's name. Amen. Heavenly Father, give me the grace to continue to live above sin and temptations, grace to forsake my old ways, grace to live your life and remain in you till I have the opportunity to meet you in Heaven. Amen."

CONGRATULATIONS!!!

You are now born again. Other things that you may need to do to grow in God are:
- Please join a Bible-based church in your city or where you live and keep growing in God
- Get a Bible and start meditating on it daily and obeying God's instructions

- Obtain help from proven believers who live Christ-like lives to guide you to know God more
- Build your relationship with the Holy Spirit – He is your spiritual mentor, guide, comforter, leader, helper and lots more
- Discover the gift that God endowed you with and use it for His glory – serve in the Church where you find yourself. Use your gift to advance the Kingdom of God
- As you keep growing, join in to win more souls for the Kingdom of God – tell other people about Jesus Christ, about the Good News of Jesus Christ.
- The journey continues….do not give up or allow the devil to deceive you.
- Be strong till the end by the authority and power that are made available to you through Jesus Christ. Use that authority and power wisely.

By His grace we shall meet in Heaven. Be blessed.

Appendix A
Why Jesus Christ Came to Earth

- To make atonement of our sins: *"In this is love, not that we loved God, but that He loved us and sent His Son to be the propitiation for our sins"*, (1 John 4:10).
- To save us from our sins and from eternal punishment: *"And she will bring forth a Son, and you shall call His name Jesus, for He will save His people from their sins."* (Matt. 1:21); *"For God so loved the world that He gave His only begotten Son, that whoever believes in Him should not perish but have everlasting life."* (John 3:16-18).
- He came to seek the lost: *"For the Son of Man has come to seek and to save that which was lost."* (Luke 19:10, Matt. 18:11)
- He came to serve: *"For even the Son of Man did not come to be served, but to serve."* (Mark 10:45).
- He came to demonstrate the true purpose of life and to give His life as a ransom: *"Just as the Son of Man did not come to be served, but to serve, and to give His life a ransom for many."* (Matt. 20:28).
- He came that all might have life more abundantly: *"I came that they may have life, and have it abundantly."* (John 10:10).

- He came to reveal the Father: *"Nor does anyone know the Father except the Son, and anyone to whom the Son wills to reveal Him"*, (Matt. 11:27). *"Jesus said to him, 'He who has seen Me has seen the Father.'"* (John 14:9).

- He came to do the will of God: *"Then He added, 'Look, I have come to do Your will.'"* (Hebrews 10:9).

- He came to proclaim, preach the Good News about the Kingdom of God and enlighten us about Heaven – The Kingdom of God: *"But He said to them, 'I must preach the kingdom of God to the other cities also, for I was sent for this purpose.'"* (Luke 4:43, Mark 1:38).

- He came to bear witness to the truth: *"For this I have come into the world, to testify to the truth. Everyone who is of the truth hears My voice"*, (John 18:37).

- He came to save sinners: *"This is a faithful saying and worthy of all acceptance, that Christ Jesus came into the world to save sinners, of whom I am chief."* (1 Timothy 1:15).

- He came into the world to be a faithful high priest: *"Therefore, in all things He had to be made like His brethren, that He might be a merciful and faithful High Priest in things pertaining to God, to make propitiation for the sins of the people."* (Hebrews 2:17).

- He came to take away sins: *"Behold, the Lamb of God who takes away the sin of the world."* (John 1:29).

- *"And you know that He was manifested to take away our sins, and in Him there is no sin."* (1 John 3:5).

- *"He then would have had to suffer often since the foundation of the world; but now, once at the end of the ages, He has appeared to put away sin by the sacrifice of Himself."* (Hebrews 9:26). He came to bear our sins: *"Who Himself bore our sins in His own body on the tree, that we, having died to sins, might live for righteousness—by whose stripes you were healed."* (1 Peter 2:24). *"So Christ was offered once to bear the sins of many. To those who eagerly wait for Him He will appear a second time, apart from sin, for salvation."* (Hebrews 9:28).

- He came to destroy the works of the devil: *"... For this purpose the Son of God was manifested, that He might destroy the works of the devil."* (1 John 3:8).

- *"Now is the judgment of this world; now the ruler of this world will be cast out."* (John 12:31). *".... for the ruler of this world is coming, and he has nothing in Me."* (John 14:30).

- *"...that through death He might destroy him who had the power of death, that is, the devil."* (Hebrews 2:14).

- He came to provide a pattern of holy living for Christians: *"because it is written, "Be holy, for I am holy."* (1 Pet. 1:16).

- Jesus Christ came into the world to be a Light in the world: *"I have come as a light into the world, that whoever believes in Me should not abide in darkness."* (John 12:46).

- Jesus Christ came into the world that all might have the abundant life: "... *I have come that they may have life, and that they may have it more abundantly.*" (John 10:10).

- Jesus Christ came into the world to judge the world: "*And Jesus said, 'For judgment I have come into this world...'*" (John 9:39).

- Jesus Christ came into the world to die on the cross: "*Now My soul is troubled, and what shall I say? 'Father, save Me from this hour'? But for this purpose I came to this hour.*" (John 12:27).

- Jesus Christ came into the world to fulfil the law: "*Do not think that I came to destroy the Law or the Prophets. I did not come to destroy but to fulfil.*" ((Matt. 5:17).

- He came to reveal and establish His Love to us and reconcile us to God: "*But God demonstrates His own love toward us, in that while we were still sinners, Christ died for us. Much more then, having now been justified by His blood, we shall be saved from wrath through Him. For if when we were enemies we were reconciled to God through the death of His Son, much more, having been reconciled, we shall be saved by His life.*" (Romans 5:8-10).

- To give us eternal life: "*And this is the testimony: that God has given us eternal life, and this life is in His Son. He who has the Son has life; he who does not have the Son of God does not have life. These things I have written to you who believe in the name of the Son of God, that you may know that you have eternal life, and that you may continue to believe in the name of the Son of God."* (1 John 5:11-13).

Appendix B

Will Those Who Have Not Heard the Gospel Be Saved?

Now, with a final question in this appendix, will those who have not heard the gospel be saved and will such people be judged for their sins or how they lived their lives on earth? This question is food for thought. There are various groups of human beings who are understood never to have heard about Jesus Christ during their lifetime. These are:

1. **Young children who have died:** It could be that they died as infants or as unborn children or as young children who could not respond to the Gospel because they did not hear it or understand it. Will they be in Heaven or Hell?

2. **Mentally incapable people:** those with mental illness or any other form of mental illness that has severe effects on their minds and which prevents them from identifying or from being able to process information effectively or correctly. How could such people hear and respond to the Gospel? Does that mean they won't go to Heaven if they do not?

3. **Old Testament people:** what about the believers in the Old Testament who had died long before Jesus Christ. What will happen to them?

4. **The present generation:** there are still people who have not still heard about the Gospel of Christ yet.

For all the people in these categories we have God's word in Deut. 1:39 and Rom. 9:11:

"*Moreover your little ones and your children, who you say will be victims, who today have no knowledge of good and evil, they shall go in there; to them I will give it, and they shall possess it.*" (Deut. 1:39 NKJV).

"*for the children not yet being born, nor having done any good or evil, that the purpose of God according to election might stand, not of works but of Him who calls.*" (Rom. 9:11 NKJV).

God's plan for these categories is not a hit-or-miss thing dependent on what people do or don't do but a sure thing determined by His decision. Hence the answer to the question, "Will they be saved?" – is in God's hands. He knows better and His words are clues too as stated in Deut. 1:39 and Rom. 9:11.

The Old Testament people are those who lived before Jesus' time including Adam, Eve, Abel, Noah, Enoch, Abraham, Sarah, Isaac, Jacob, Moses, Joshua, Joseph, Samuel, David, Elijah, Rahab, Gideon. These and other unknown people who believed in God, who by faith became righteous and obtained the promise will enter the Kingdom of God: (Matt. 8:10-11, Luke 9:27-31, Luke 13:28-29, Luke 16:22-25, Romans 4:1-8, Heb. 11:4-32).

How will people be judged?

As we grow up in life and at a point in our lives we will be able to understand and be able to identify what is right from what is wrong, we can distinguish right from wrong; right friendships from wrong friendships; right habits from bad habits; right places to visit from wrong places to visit. We can distinguish a right lifestyle from a wrong lifestyle and much more. These Scriptures passages also give clarity to what is right from what is wrong (Mark 7:20-23, 1 Cor. 6:9-11, 1 Cor. 15:33, 1 John 2:15-17, James 4:17).

Since we know what is right from what is wrong, we will have no excuse why we end up in the side of eternal location – Heaven or Hell based on the type of decisions and choices we make on earth. The types of decisions (to accept Jesus Christ or not to) and choices (right or bad) we make on earth with what we do with our lives are very important as the true character of our works will be exposed before the eyes of the saviour. Works – our labours on earth, what we do on earth, our personal assignment, what we accomplish at the end of our lives. The entirety of our life. Do remember the parable of the talents in Matt. 25:14-30.

This parable also gives us a foretaste of how the judgment of God would be to all humanity and it also affirms the fact that we all have been given one talent in order to fulfil our potential, to reach our goals and purpose in life. It is an indication that the life we live and the talent that we have is given to us by God, one that we are supposed to use for His glory, to win more souls for Him: to evangelize and preach the Gospel and to expand God's Kingdom on earth. We use that talent to enlighten others at our work places, in our neighbourhood, schools, universities, colleges, airports, and everywhere we can as long as we abide by the law. We are meant to use it to glorify God and to help others. We have got to discover the talent that we have and use it wisely, efficiently and effectively for God.

Now, pondering on this Scripture (Matt. 25:14-30) this is what it is like in the Kingdom of Heaven; this is what judgment is like in Heaven. So, whoever is judged and condemned to Hell cannot claim that the decision or sentence is unfair or unjust. The servant who hides the talent in the ground represents people who find excuses to why they are living a wayward life or try to justify why they do the sinful things they do or to justify their sins or find fault with the Gospel, have issues with churches or church structures or leadership; they complain about most things or why God should have done A or B or C for them. The list goes on and on. If we belong to this category, it is high time we stop complaining and murmuring (Phil 2:14, James 5:9, Eph. 4:29), but appreciate God in all things (1 Thess. 5:18) and stop complaining about our life and stop comparing our life or ourselves with others (2 Cor. 10:12, Gal. 6:4-5, Gal. 1:10, 1 Thess. 4:11-12). God has made each of us special and talented (1 Peter 2:9), to discover and understand who we are and what we are meant to accomplish on earth and for His glory. If we have been doing it, we must not give up or allow distractions. We should focus on our vision and our purpose to accomplish what we have started and to finish the race with patience – just like Paul:

"I have fought the good fight, I have finished the race, I have kept the faith. Finally, there is laid up for me the crown of righteousness, which the Lord, the righteous

Judge, will give to me on that Day, and not to me only but also to all who have loved His appearing." (2 Tim. 4:7-8 NKJV).

Paul finished the race and kept the faith. In the Kingdom of God, there are rewards for those who faithfully finish the race and keep the faith.

However, the servant who hid the talent in the ground probably thought life on earth was mainly about partying, enjoying and having fun. He did not realise that the life given was to be spent in a way that would bring good results, a life used wisely, used rightfully.

In summary, whoever is judged and condemned to Hell cannot claim that the judgment is unjust (Rom. 1:18-21, Rev. 20:11-15).

Now, where would you like to spend eternity – Heaven or Hell? If you have made up our minds, is there anything in your life today that you need to get rid of? Attitudes? The way you speak? Anger? Hatred? and as the list goes on and on:

"Now the works of the flesh are evident, which are: adultery, fornication, uncleanness, lewdness, idolatry, sorcery, hatred, contentions, jealousies, outbursts of wrath, selfish ambitions, dissensions, heresies, envy, murders, drunkenness, revelries, and the like; of which I tell you beforehand, just as I also told you in time past, that those who practice such things will not inherit the kingdom of God." (Gal. 5:19-21 NKJV).

Will it not be good to start preparing for your eternal placement – your eternal home, Heaven, right now?

And is there anything you feel or discover in your life as a whole that may hinder your desired eternal placement? Why don't you make up your mind, be determined to make a clean break with such sin, let go of sinful ways, lifestyles that do not bring honour and glory to God, stop making bad choices and wrong decisions which can only lead to the wrong eternal placement. Stop blaming others or circumstances but, '...*be sure your sin will find you out*' (Num. 32:23). Do remember that Hell is in fact not a nice place in the first place, a place of torment, a place where its fire never burns out but increases (Matt. 22:13, Mark 9:43-48). In Hell, there is no salvation, It is a lonely place, no social life, not partying as un-ending pain and anguish is the order of the eternal day there, no change of heart or mind, no change of choices or decisions, no more change of location because it is a realm of permanence. No more changes, everything there is forever.

This may be the only final opportunity to gain access to Heaven. It is only through Jesus Christ. Why can't you accept Him today? Why can't you say this prayer?

"Lord Jesus, I repent of my sins, I confess all my sins (*mention each* ...), and I ask for your forgiveness Lord Jesus. Come into my heart, come in today, come in to stay and I make you my Lord and Saviour in Jesus' name. Amen".

Congratulations! Find a Bible-based Church to continue to develop your relationship with God and be mentored by proven believers and seek further help by water baptism, being filled with the Holy Spirit, living a life of faith and learning how to exercise agape love always, and how to continue to do the will of the Heavenly Father on a daily basis till the end. You have positioned yourself from now on for the right eternal placement – Heaven:

"He who has an ear, let him hear what the Spirit says to the churches. To him who overcomes I will give to eat from the tree of life, which is in the midst of the Paradise of God." (Rev. 2:7 NKJV).

While on the other hand, Heaven is in fact a beautiful place with mansions (John 14:2), a peaceful, holy and perfect place (Rev.21:1-2,27, Matt. 5:48). The construction of its wall is of jasper, and the city is pure gold like clear glass, while the foundations of the wall of the city are adorned with all kinds of precious stones (Rev. 21:14-21).

This, moreover, is for those who live a Christ-like life:

"But as it is written:
"Eye has not seen, nor ear heard,
Nor have entered into the heart of man
The things which God has prepared
for those who love Him." (1 Cor. 2:9 NKJV).

Appendix C

Judgements:
Judgement Seat of Christ and the Final Judgement

"For we must all appear before the judgment seat of Christ, that each one may receive the things done in the body, according to what he has done, whether good or bad." (2 Cor. 5:10 NKJV)

"Then I saw a great white throne and Him who sat on it, from whose face the earth and the heaven fled away. And there was found no place for them. And I saw the dead, small and great, standing before God, and books were opened. And another book was opened, which is the Book of Life. And the dead were judged according to their works, by the things which were written in the books." (Rev. 20:11-12 NKJV).

Righteous believers will be judged at the Judgement seat of Christ (2 Cor. 5:10) where they will be judged and be rewarded. This sort of judgement is not about deciding their eternal placement but it will be a judgement for rewards, for their names will already be in the Book of Life. Righteous believers' works cannot save them but their deeds, accomplishments are important to God (1 Cor. 3:11-15).

It is imperative also to note that the unrighteous also will be judged according to their works. And this is the judgement at *"the great white throne"* (Rev. 20:11-15). This must not be confused with judgment seat of Christ (2 Cor. 5:10). But, of course, no works, no matter how good, will be able to save them. Only the unrighteous will be at this judgement and there are no rewards. It is important to note that God does not send anyone to Hell: they made such choice by rejecting Jesus Christ, the Saviour (John 3:16-21). In other words, they send themselves to Hell through their wrong choices – with their own sovereign will power. Hence, human beings must make a choice while on earth as to where he or she would like to spend eternity: Heaven or Hell? This is why this book is timely and very important in reminding every human being of the urgency of making the right choice of eternal home – Heaven before it is too late. God's Judgment is complete as death and Hell will be thrown into the lake of fire. This is the second death – the Lake of Fire.

One of the ironies of the concept of Heaven or Hell is that if you die, you die alone and when you stand before the judgement seat of Christ, you will stand alone to give an account of what you have done in the body, to give an account of what you have done on earth alone, either fulfilled or un-fulfilled, good or bad, acceptable or not acceptable. You would not have your friends or social network friends; you would not have your parents, wife or husband, siblings, mentors, pastors, prayer partners, colleagues who will stand there with you. You will have to face the judgement alone. And one of the imperatives that distinguishes Hell from Heaven is loneliness. Here on earth we have friends and relationships as part of our social life, but in Hell the reverse is the case. Such loneliness — and sadly it is forever.

However, the judgement seat of Christ is about rewarding faithful stewards, faithful Christians, righteous believers for how they have lived on earth – good or bad and to be rewarded accordingly. This does not determine eternal location or eternal placement – Heaven or Hell. Here is a further explanation regarding the Judgement seat of Christ as expounded by two authors:

"The judgment seat of Christ will be a place of revelation, as we 'stand before Christ to be judged'. As we live and work here on earth, it is relatively easy for us to hide things and pretend; but the true character of our works will be exposed before the searching eyes of the saviour. He will reveal whether our works have been good or evil. The character of our service will be revealed (1 Cor. 3:13) as well as the motives that impelled us (1 Cor. 4:5). It will also be a place of reckoning, as we give account of our ministries." (Rom. 14:10-12) (Dr Warren W. Wiersbe, The Transformation Study Bible, p. 1964).

"… but Christians' lives will still be judged by Christ. Salvation is never obtained by works (Rom. 4:4-5), and this judgement before Christ will not determine believers' eternal destiny. Instead, at this judgement, Christ will reward Christians for how they have lived on earth. God's gracious gift of salvation does not free Christians from the requirement of faithful obedience to Christ. All Christians must give an account for how they have lived in this body." (The life application New Testament Commentary, p. 727).